Strategies for Teaching Assistant and International Teaching Assistant Development

Strategies for Teaching Assistant and International Teaching Assistant Development

BEYOND MICRO TEACHING

Catherine **Ross**, Jane **Dunphy**, and Associates

JOSSEY-BASS
A Wiley Imprint
www.josseybass.com

Published by Jossey-Bass
A Wiley Imprint
989 Market Street, San Francisco, CA 94103–1741
www.josseybass.com

Jossey-Bass books and products are available through most bookstores. To contact Jossey-Bass directly call our Customer Care Department within the U.S. at 800-956-7739, outside the U.S. at 317-572-3986, or fax 317-572-4002.

Jossey-Bass also publishes its books in a variety of electronic formats. Some content that appears in print may not be available in electronic books.

Library of Congress Cataloging-in-Publication Data

Ross, Catherine, 1955-
   Strategies for teaching assistant and international teaching assistant development : beyond micro teaching / Catherine Ross, Jane Dunphy, and associates. — 1st ed.
      p. cm.
   Includes bibliographical references and index.
   ISBN 978-0-470-18082-2 (cloth)
   1. Graduate teaching assistants—Training of—United States. 2. Teachers, Foreign—Training of—United States. I. Dunphy, Jane, 1956- II. Title.
   LB2335.4.R67 2007
   378.1'25—dc22   2007026432

Printed in the United States of America
FIRST EDITION
HB Printing 10 9 8 7 6 5 4 3 2 1

We dedicate this book to our inspirational mentors,
to our phenomenal colleagues, and to our remarkable
students, from whom we have learned so much.

TABLE OF **CONTENTS**

ABOUT THE **AUTHORS**

Gabriele Bauer is assistant director of the Center for Teaching Effectiveness at the University of Delaware. In this role she directs the teaching certification program for graduate students, coordinates teaching assistant (TA) training services, and consults with faculty and departments on aspects of student learning and instructional enhancement. She received her Ph.D. at Penn State in speech communication with emphases on ESL and instructional supervision. Her research interests focus on the professional development of graduate TAs and the evaluation of teaching effectiveness.

Jill Bible is a head teaching assistant for the Earth Systems Program at Stanford University. She assists in a senior seminar and co-coordinates a large introductory class that emphasizes an interdisciplinary approach to environmental issues. Jill received her B.S. in earth systems from Stanford in 2004 and will receive her M.S. in earth systems from Stanford in 2007. She concentrates on communication and education about environmental issues and has worked with the Center for Teaching and Learning at Stanford, leading workshops on interdisciplinary teaching.

Lori Breslow has directed the Teaching and Learning Lab at the Massachusetts Institute of Technology since its inception in 1997. She teaches a yearly doctoral-level course on teaching science and engineering in the university. In addition, she is a senior lecturer in professional and managerial communication at the Sloan School of Management. Her research interests include interdisciplinary education and dissemination of educational innovation.

Derek Bruff is a teaching assistant and faculty developer at the Vanderbilt University Center for Teaching, consulting with instructors from across the university and facilitating workshops and other programs on teaching and learning issues. He has a Ph.D. in mathematics from Vanderbilt and taught at Harvard University before returning to Vanderbilt in 2005, where he continues to teach in the mathematics department.

Vel Chesser is a consultant for the Graduate School at Syracuse University where she assists in coordinating research projects related to the Future Professoriate Program and English language services.

Marcelo Clerici-Arias has been associate director for social sciences and technology at the Center for Teaching and Learning at Stanford University since 2001. From 1996–1997 he was an assistant professor at the Universidad de San Andrés in Argentina. In 1998 he came to Stanford as the associate director of the Introductory Economics Center before moving to the Center for Teaching and Learning. He continues teaching in the Department of Economics, and he is the Resident Fellow in Cedro, one of Stanford's undergraduate residences.

Mark Decker is a doctoral candidate in the Department of Educational Psychology at the University of Texas at Austin (UT–Austin). He holds a B.A. in English and psychology from Texas Tech and a master's degree in social work from UT–Austin with an emphasis in administration and planning. He has been the Graduate Student Instructor program coordinator since 2004. Prior to that, he led the Center for Instructional Technologies' (CIT) Courseware Group, providing training, support, and consulting for web course development tools such as WebCT and Blackboard. While with CIT, Mark presented at regional and national instructional technology conferences.

Mariatte Denman is associate director for the humanities at the Center for Teaching and Learning (CTL) at Stanford University. She holds a B.A. in education and literature and a teaching credential from the University of Berne in Switzerland, and a Ph.D. in German with designated emphases in critical theory and feminist research and theory from the University of California–Davis. Prior to coming to CTL in 2004, she was a postdoctoral teaching fellow in the humanities at Stanford and an assistant professor in

German studies at Duke University. At CTL, Mariatte consults with faculty and graduate students on teaching and professional development, conducts mid-quarter small group evaluations, and offers teaching and professional development workshops in humanities departments and for the general campus.

Jennie Dorman is a senior consultant in the Center for Instructional Development and Research (CIDR) at the University of Washington where she consults with faculty and teaching assistants (TAs) from the social sciences and STEM (science, technology, engineering, and mathematics) disciplines. In addition to consulting, she directs the ongoing development of workshop materials for CIDR's annual TA training conference and teaches an interdisciplinary graduate course on Teaching and Learning in Higher Education. Jennie is particularly interested in helping instructors find feasible and meaningful ways to integrate writing into their courses. She received a B.A. in political science from the University of California–Berkeley and a Ph.D. in molecular and cellular biology from the University of Washington.

Robyn Wright Dunbar is senior associate director for science and engineering at the Center for Teaching and Learning at Stanford University, where she is also associate professor, by courtesy, of geological and environmental sciences. She earned her Ph.D. in geology from Rice University in 1984 and taught geology at the University of New Mexico and Rice University prior to coming to Stanford in 1998. At Stanford, she consults with faculty and graduate students on teaching and curriculum, leads teaching and academic career development workshops and summer institutes, and teaches courses in science and engineering pedagogy, as well as introductory geology.

Jane Dunphy has taught academic and professional communication, as well as English, in the humanities department and at the Sloan School of Management at the Massachusetts Institute of Technology (MIT) since 1981. Beyond her regular teaching and administrative duties as director of English Language Studies, she is involved in working with MIT's Teaching and Learning Lab to provide support to teaching assistants and faculty members through workshops, seminars, consultations, and courses; designing and facilitating seminars in academic and professional communication for various departments and communities at MIT and at Woods Hole Oceanographic Institute; and consulting in professional communications to corporations and universities in the United States and abroad. Her research interests focus on best practices in professional communication protocols across cultures.

Phillip M. Edwards is an instructional consultant at the Center for Instructional Development and Research (CIDR) at the University of Washington (UW) where he is also a doctoral candidate in information science at the UW Information School. He received an M.S. in information (2003) from the University of Michigan and a B.S. in chemistry with a minor in mathematics (2001) from the University at Buffalo–SUNY. At CIDR, he consults with teaching assistants from the sciences, mathematics, and engineering. In addition to his disciplinary research interests in open access publishing and scholarly communication, Phillip is especially interested in pedagogical uses of technology inside and outside of the classroom, mentoring graduate and undergraduate students, and classroom assessment techniques.

Karen Freisem is a senior consultant in the Center for Instructional Development and Research (CIDR) at the University of Washington where she works primarily with the math, science, and engineering departments. She consults with individual faculty and teaching assistants (TAs) on issues of teaching and learning. In addition, she assists departments in planning and implementing program assessment, and she designs and facilitates workshops for groups of faculty and TAs. For 10 years before joining CIDR in 1986, Karen developed curriculum and taught in a variety of settings. Her current research interests focus on student perceptions of effective instruction in large classes. She has two master's degrees from the University of Washington, one in Slavic linguistics and the other in TESOL.

Judith Gibber, a biologist, is the former director of the Graduate School of Arts and Science Teaching Center at Columbia University.

Janet Goodwin is a lecturer in the Department of Applied Linguistics and TESL at the University of California–Los Angeles. In addition to training international teaching assistants, she teaches a variety of ESL and teacher education courses. One of her primary interests is the intersection of discourse, prosody, and body movement. She is coauthor of *Teaching Pronunciation: A Reference for Teachers of English to Speakers of Other Languages* (Cambridge University Press, 1996).

Barbara Gourlay coordinates the English for International Teaching Assistants Program at Brown University. Her research interests include technology in second language teaching and learning and intercultural communication in academic settings.

Stacy Grooters is a Ph.D. candidate in English at the University of Washington (UW) where she is finishing a dissertation on narratives of education in colonial and postcolonial literature. At UW, she served as an instructional consultant in the Center for Instructional Development and Research and has taught in the departments of English, American ethnic studies, and women studies. In 2007 she began work as founding director of the Center for Teaching and Learning at Stonehill College in Massachusetts.

Anne Halbert is the international teaching assistant (ITA) coordinator for the Teaching Assistant Program at the University of Connecticut. She has been teaching and developing ITA courses since receiving her master's degree in linguistics from the University of Connecticut in 1997.

Joe Hannah recently completed his Ph.D. in geography at the University of Washington. He received an M.A. in Asian studies at Cornell University (1989) and a B.S. in international agricultural development from the University of California–Davis (1995). In addition to his research interests in political geography, Joe has assisted in teaching a number of lab classes in geographic information systems and critical cartography. He has an ongoing interest in developing computer lab-based pedagogies and has developed course materials for both technical and nontechnical classes.

Shaun K. Kane is a Ph.D. candidate in the Information School at the University of Washington (UW). His research interests include assistive technology, end-user programming, and design education. He has taught courses on information design, programming, and web technology. Shaun served as facilitator for the workshop Teaching in Computer Lab Settings: First Day and Beyond at UW's 2006 TA Conference on Teaching and Learning. He holds an M.S. in computer science from the University of Massachusetts Amherst.

Kimberly Kenyon is assistant director of the International Teaching Assistant Development Program at Cornell University. She has been interested in ESL since 1984 and has worked as an ESL instructor at the State University of New York at Albany as well as in Japan, China, Hawaii, and Thailand. She holds two M.S. degrees from the State University of New York at Albany in curriculum design and instructional technology and TESOL. She is currently in the dissertation process of her Ph.D. in curriculum design and instructional technology at the State University of New York at Albany.

Margaret Lawrence is a senior consultant in the Center for Instructional Development and Research (CIDR) at the University of Washington and coordinator of CIDR's work with departments in social sciences, arts and humanities, and some professional schools. In addition to consulting, Margaret has helped develop CIDR materials on a variety of topics including peer observation, active learning, motivation, and foreign language teaching. She is especially interested in teacher beliefs: How instructors arrive at the beliefs they hold about teaching and learning and the outworking of those beliefs in instructional practices. She also works with teaching assistants in CIDR's International TA Program.

Christine Liptak received a B.A. in cultural anthropology and is completing her M.A. in ESL at the University of Minnesota. She has experience teaching in Austria, France, and China, and taught as an apprentice in the ITA Program at the University of Minnesota.

Michele Marincovich is associate vice provost for undergraduate education and director of the Center for Teaching and Learning at Stanford University. Shortly after finishing her Ph.D. in history, she joined the center as assistant director and initiated the campus's first videotaping and consultation programs for teaching assistants (TAs). With a fellow lecturer from the Department of Linguistics, she also inaugurated Stanford's first course on teaching for international TAs. Since 1979 she has concentrated on work with faculty as well; her efforts in both teaching and learning improvement in 1988 brought her the university's prestigious Dinkelspiel Award for Outstanding Service to Undergraduate Education. Equally active off campus, Michele is a past president of the Professional and Organizational Development Network in Higher Education and a frequent presenter at campuses and conferences in the United States and abroad. She is coauthor of *Disciplinary Differences in Teaching and Learning: Implications for Practice* (Jossey-Bass, 1995) and *The Professional Development of Graduate Teaching Assistants* (Anker, 1998).

Allyson Polsky McCabe is former director of Johns Hopkins Teaching Assistant Training Institute. She presently teaches English at Yale University, where she also serves as the associate course director of Writing Seminars I.

Nancy C. McClure is founding director of the Center for Teaching Excellence at Fairmont State University where she designs professional development activities for more than 500 full-time and part-time faculty. In addition to providing faculty with these opportunities, Nancy consults with individual faculty on their endeavors to excel at teaching. She has authored many professional publications for both high school and college faculty, including 12 resource units and a commissioned essay published for college English teachers by the Gale Group, and four articles on teaching and learning for the POD–IDEA Center Notes and Learning Papers Projects. She regularly presents on teaching and learning at local, regional, and national conferences. She also has a freelance writing and consulting business that has served 19 education clients since 1996. As a professor of education, Nancy holds a Ph.D. in curriculum and instruction and worked from 1986–2002 as a teacher educator.

Colleen Meyers teaches in the Center for Teaching and Learning at the University of Minnesota. She is coauthor of *Communicate: Strategies for International Teaching Assistants* (Pearson, 1992) and the *Pronunciation for Success* teacher-training materials and self-study course. She has more than 20 years' experience working with international teaching assistants.

Kyoung-Ah Nam is completing her Ph.D. at the University of Minnesota where she teaches Korean language and the Maximizing Study Abroad course as an international teaching assistant. Prior to entering the doctoral program she worked for more than 10 years with international organizations and media including the UN, UNESCO, Ogilvy and Mather, Mindshare, Samsung, and Radio Free Asia. Her research interests include aspects of the link between language and culture and effective training in intercultural communication.

Sara O'Brien is a graduate student in the biology department at the University of Washington (UW). Her doctoral thesis will examine the neuroendocrine influences on breeding flexibility in birds. She has held teaching assistantships for a variety of biology classes at UW, and has served as a workshop facilitator for UW's annual multidisciplinary teaching assistant training conference on topics relating to effective teaching in laboratory settings and discussion sections. Sara is also exploring science writing and continues to take classes in technical communications. She received a B.S. in animal science and an M.S. in integrative biology from the University of Illinois, Champaign–Urbana.

Theresa L. Pettit is director of the International Teaching Assistant Development Program at Cornell University. Prior to assuming this position in 2002, she was an assistant professor of ESL education and French at Cortland State University. She has held adjunct faculty positions in ESL, Spanish, and foreign language education at Syracuse University, Oswego State University, and Madison Area Technical College. In addition, she taught Spanish and French at the secondary school level for more than 20 years. Theresa holds a B.S. and M.A. in foreign language education from the Ohio State University and a doctor of arts degree in foreign languages and ESL from Syracuse University.

Tershia Pinder joined the Center for Research on Learning in Teaching (CRLT) at the University of Michigan (U–M) in August 2005. After receiving a B.S. in fire protection engineering from the University of Maryland, she went on to earn an M.S. and Ph.D. in mechanical engineering from the University of Michigan. In addition to numerous academic and leadership awards, Tershia received the National Collegiate Engineering Award and the U–M ScholarPower Ph.D. Student Achievement Award. She has been a graduate student instructor (GSI) and a College of Engineering GSI Mentor. In her role at CRLT, Tershia is responsible for administering midterm student feedback sessions, overseeing Engineering GSI Mentor training, facilitating the Preparing Future Faculty Seminar, and planning GSI Teacher Training in the College of Engineering.

Pamela Pollock, a Ph.D. candidate in education at Cornell University, has been an international teaching assistant trainer for more than five years. She is also a teaching assistant for Cornell's International Teaching Assistant Development Program, part of the Center for Learning and Teaching. Pamela has a B.A. in Spanish literature from Bryn Mawr College and an M.A. in foreign language education and applied linguistics from the University of Texas at Austin.

Janet Rankin is associate professor of engineering at Brown University where she teaches a variety of materials science courses as well as general courses in the engineering core. She received her Sc.B. in engineering from Brown University in 1983 and her Ph.D. in materials science and engineering from the Massachusetts Institute of Technology in 1989. From 1989–1991, Janet was a staff scientist at Oak Ridge National Lab, and a Bunting Fellow at Radcliffe College from 1991–1992. She received a Visiting Professorship for Women Award from the National Science Foundation, which funded her research at Brown from 1993–1995. Her current research is supported by grants from the National Science Foundation and the U.S. Department of Energy. From 1998–2000, Janet was coordinator of Brown's ExSEL Program, which supports and encourages the participation of traditionally underrepresented minorities in math and science disciplines.

Catherine Ross received her Ph.D. in Russian from the University of Texas and two master's degrees (TESL and Russian) from the University of Wisconsin. Since 1998 she has held several positions at the University of Connecticut, where she is presently associate director of the Institute for Teaching and Learning and director of Teaching Assistant Programs. She works with faculty, teaching assistants (TAs), and international teaching assistants (ITAs) from all disciplines, both individually and in workshops and orientations. She has produced a video for training ITAs, *Respect on the Line,* and has published a chapter, "From Complaints to Communication," in the TESOL Case Studies in Practice Series, *Professional Development of International Teaching Assistants.* In addition to her regular administrative and faculty development duties, she has spent hundreds of hours observing and troubleshooting the classroom teaching of TAs and faculty at the University of Connecticut, across a wide variety of disciplines. She is past chair of the International Teaching Assistant Interest Section in TESOL and cofounder of the New England ITA Network, which includes Harvard, Yale, Brown, MIT, the University of Massachusetts, the University of Rhode Island, and Worcester Polytechnic Institute. She is a frequent presenter at TESOL, most recently presenting research around undergraduate attitudes toward ITAs.

Margo Sampson is the ESOL language coordinator at Syracuse University. She has been involved with the training and instruction of international teaching assistants since 1991.

J. Mark Schuster is professor of urban cultural policy in the Department of Urban Studies and Planning at the Massachusetts Institute of Technology. His research interests include cultural and urban design policy and qualitative and quantitative methods.

Shawna Shapiro has taught English, ESOL, social studies, and Spanish at the middle school, high school, and university levels. She is presently completing a Ph.D. in language and rhetoric at the University of Washington, specializing in second language writing.

Doris Yaffe Shiffman has been teaching in and coordinating the ESL Program for International TAs at Johns Hopkins University since 1989. Before that she taught ESL at Towson University and in the Baltimore County Adult Education Program. She holds a bachelor's degree from Brandeis University, a permanent teaching credential earned at the University of California–Berkeley, and a master's degree from Johns Hopkins University. She has presented at TESOL, WATESOL, MATESOL, NEITAN, and MAITA. Her special areas of interest are pronunciation and using technology to enhance the effectiveness of working with international teaching assistants.

Michelle Smith recently began a science teaching fellow position at the University of Colorado–Boulder working in the molecular cellular and developmental biology department. Presently she is developing new methods of assessment and active learning activities in the undergraduate genetics course. In addition, Michelle is conducting research on the roles of class size and formal and informal peer interactions on student performance and perception of success. She holds a Ph.D. in zoology from the University of Washington, an M.S. in biology from the University of Dayton, and a B.A. in biology from Hanover College.

Elena Stetsenko works at the Center for Teaching and Learning at the University of Minnesota. She was educated in Russia, Ukraine, and Great Britain. She works with international teaching assistants and international faculty, and her goal is to help students learn teaching practices that will help them to be successful global teachers.

Barbara Thompson teaches pedagogy, oral language, and presentation skills to international graduate students who may become teaching assistants at Princeton University.

Stacey Lane Tice is associate dean of the Graduate School and director of the TA Program and Future Professoriate Program at Syracuse University. She is co-editor of *Preparing Graduate Students to Teach: A Guide to Programs that Improve Undergraduate Education and Develop Tomorrow's Faculty* (Stylus, 1993) and *University Teaching: A Guide for Graduate Students* (Syracuse University Press, 1996), as well as several articles related to preparing graduate students for faculty positions.

Lee Warren is associate director of the Derek Bok Center for Teaching and Learning at Harvard University. She is a pedagogical coach for faculty and graduate students teaching in the undergraduate college. Her particular interests include race, gender, and class in the classroom; case teaching; and leadership. She has written numerous articles on these subjects and produced two videos: *Race in the Classroom* and *Women in the Classroom.*

Elizabeth Wittner is academic director of the Center for American English Language and Culture and the ITA Program coordinator for the Teaching Resource Center at the University of Virginia. As part of her work at the university, Elizabeth runs a volunteer program in which undergraduates work as teaching, classroom, and language partners. In addition to working with university students, she has worked with migrant families, in adult education, and in K–12 education as a classroom teacher and teacher educator. Her interests include cross-cultural communication, pronunciation, and pedagogy.

Mary C. Wright is an assistant research scientist at the Center for Research on Learning and Teaching (CRLT) at the University of Michigan (U–M). She has an A.B. in sociology from Princeton University, an M.A. and Ph.D. in sociology from U–M, and an M.A. in higher education administration from U–M's Center for the Study of Higher and Postsecondary Education. Her work at CRLT focuses on Preparing Future Faculty initiatives and Graduate Student Instructor programs. Her book, *Always at Odds? Creating Alignment Between Faculty and Administrative Values,* is forthcoming from SUNY Press.

Lu Zhang is a Ph.D. candidate in the Department of Sociology at Johns Hopkins University (JHU). She served as a doctoral intern in the university's teaching assistant (TA) training program at the Center for Education Resources during 2005–2006. For three courses she was a TA, and has worked closely with the Office of Academics at JHU as a tutor and study consultant for undergraduates. Lu is interested in labor studies, China studies, and international development; her dissertation is about globalization, market reform, and the dynamics of labor unrest in China since 1980 through a case study of the Chinese automobile industry. She is presently doing her fieldwork at eight automobile plants in China with the support of a Social Science Research Council Fellowship and National Science Foundation Grant.

FOREWORD

The last 25 years have seen the creation and expansion of programs to support graduate teaching assistants (TAs) in the academy. In large part, this young field has arisen in response to public concerns about rising tuition and increasing numbers of untrained graduate students taking on the responsibility of teaching undergraduates. As the public calls for accountability increased, institutions of higher education began to examine their responsibility to provide high-quality education to all students. There is now evidence that some educators are starting to address the professional communication and teaching skills of graduate students, an important factor in both the undergraduate courses being taught and in graduate education. Given that teaching assistantships represent a significant financial commitment on the part of institutions, and that the future of our higher education faculty rests on these students, it is important that TAs are the recipients of appropriate orientation, mentoring, and ongoing professional development.

Happily, the efforts of professionals in the field of TA development are increasingly supported by publications that provide related research on teaching and learning, models and frameworks for TA programs, and plans for program implementation. Scholars have even started to explore the short history of TA development in the United States. We have, then, a growing body of literature that explains the "what, why, and when" of the field. But there are few publications that explain "how" to help TAs and international TAs learn the skills that they need to provide effective instruction to undergraduates.

Thanks to the shared vision of Jane Dunphy and Catherine Ross, we now have a new and exceptional resource that provides practical, motivating, and effective techniques drawn from programs across the country. *Strategies for Teaching Assistant and International Teaching Assistant Development* will help educators foster the discrete communication skills that graduate students need to teach, mentor, and develop as professionals.

Stacey Lane Tice
Associate Dean of the Graduate School
Syracuse University

PREFACE

Strategies for Teaching Assistant and International Teaching Assistant Development: Beyond Micro Teaching is a resource for anyone who works with graduate students to support their teaching efforts in American research universities. You may work as a program director who serves as an institute-wide resource, responsible for developing fall orientation workshops or monthly seminars for graduate teaching assistants (TAs). Or you may be a department-based teaching expert, even a head TA, who focuses on orientating new TAs to the teaching practices of a specific discipline. Perhaps your focus is international teaching assistants (ITAs), and you must address language and cultural issues in addition to pedagogical concerns.

Whether you are choosing techniques for your orientation schedule or facilitating the techniques in workshop or classroom sessions, your responsibilities vary widely, but your major goal is the same: preparing graduate students for success in their teaching and mentoring responsibilities. Effective TAs require relatively sophisticated communication skills. They must know how to present information in a digestible form, foster and manage classroom interactions, and conduct lab sessions. They are expected to engage appropriately in small talk and other rapport-building techniques. In addition, they require the sensitivity to be effective in office hours, and to understand and handle diversity issues. As an administrator, facilitator, or instructor, your job is to ensure that the TAs with whom you work receive the instruction, practice, and feedback necessary to succeed.

Micro teaching—a short, recorded lesson delivered by a novice teacher, followed by analysis and discussion of the recording with an expert teacher—is widely used, and in some cases is the only activity used, in TA training. It is a beneficial but limited technique. Before choreographing the various steps of a micro lesson, many TAs need focused instruction and practice in the discrete elements that come together to form that lesson, such as framing a topic, developing an explanation from the concrete to the more abstract, using visual aids effectively, or eliciting and managing interactions with students. In addition, ITAs require activities to help them develop cultural understanding and linguistic flexibility—exercises far outside the scope of traditional micro teaching.

Regional and national conferences, such as the Professional and Organizational Development Network and Teachers of English to Speakers of Other Languages, provide opportunities for the exchange of ideas and practices for TA development that go beyond micro teaching. However, few of these techniques have been collected or disseminated in published form since the mid 1990s.

This book draws on the extensive experience of many professional educators who represent a variety of programs throughout the United States. The contributors understand the common constraints of many TA development classes, workshops, or programs: limited budget, staff, and time; overextended graduate students; underinvolved faculty; and increased public concern about the role of TAs and ITAs in the academy. They share, with all professionals in the field, the need for sophisticated techniques that motivate and are practical and focused. Their contributions to this book have proven effective in developing the sophisticated communication skills required by TAs across the disciplines.

This book is divided into two parts. The first part provides activities to foster confidence and teaching skills in novices, as well as strategies for more experienced TAs to refine their skills and develop as educators outside the classroom. The second part addresses the particular needs of international TAs with a variety of techniques to promote linguistic, cultural, and pedagogical ease in the American academy. Many of the 45 activities found here include variations that make them suitable for wider or narrower audiences, or for repeated use with the same audience.

Catherine Ross
University of Connecticut

Jane Dunphy
Massachusetts Institute of Technology

January 2007

ACKNOWLEDGMENTS

Special thanks to members of our New England ITA Network for their enthusiasm and willingness to share. And a very special thanks to Maria Hramiak whose good nature and outstanding technical and organizational skills kept this project alive and moving forward, and to Ashley Viens for hours of proofreading and final manuscript production.

PART ONE

TA Development

CHAPTER **ONE**

Getting Started

Too often, graduate students react to their new teaching assistant (TA) status with paralyzing trepidation or cocky overconfidence. The most efficient way to help them find the balance they need is to provide opportunities to examine their assumptions and expectations. Many factors that contribute to effective teaching are based on common sense—for example, planning ahead, understanding your audience and yourself, presenting information in digestible chunks, creating a welcoming classroom environment, and learning your department and university policies. Still, novice TAs benefit enormously from explicit treatment of these topics and purposeful practice of the associated skills. The techniques presented in Chapter 1 provide a variety of ways to cover "Teaching 101."

Acknowledging Teaching Fears: The Three-Minute Free Response

Janet Rankin

Brown University

GOALS
- To help TAs acknowledge their concerns about teaching and mentoring
- To help TAs develop strategies to address those concerns

PREPARATION TIME

None

EXECUTION TIME
- 10 minutes to introduce the exercise and to distribute, formulate, and collect responses
- The time necessary for discussion of responses varies depending on the size of the group.

ASSUMPTIONS

All participants will be working as TAs in the near future.

RESOURCES

3 x 5 index cards

Introduction

First-time and even veteran TAs are often extremely apprehensive about the TA experience in the classroom or lab. This activity addresses TA concerns in a supportive environment and can help allay many fears. In addition, the exercise models a technique that TAs will be able to use in their own classroom teaching.

Procedure

1. At the beginning of either a department-based or institute/university-wide TA training session, each student is given two 3 x 5 index cards and asked to anonymously answer the following two questions:
   - With respect to TAing, what are two things about which you are most fearful, apprehensive, or anxious (one item/side)?
   - With respect to TAing, what are two things about which you are most excited (one item/side)?

2. Students are given sufficient time to answer these questions, then the cards are collected. The training facilitator then chooses representative statements (positive and negative) and asks the group for reactions to the comments.

3. The group discusses possible strategies for dealing with the stated fears/concerns.

Outcomes

Often, multiple students express a similar concern. Consequently, verbalizing a concern and discussing possible solutions as a group provides students with concrete approaches for addressing the issue and shows students that most concerns are shared by many. It is useful for the facilitator to comment when a particular issue has been identified by multiple participants. Sharing the "positive" responses can help to motivate apprehensive students.

When this technique is used in department-based trainings, student fears may be quite specific ("I'm afraid that when I try to run the _____ piece of equipment, it will not work, and the student lab/data will be ruined."). Such specific fears can often be addressed by connecting apprehensive students with more experienced TAs from the department or by encouraging or facilitating more TA-faculty contact.

When this technique is implemented in cross-departmental trainings, TAs have the opportunity to learn how students from other departments deal with specific situations. These solutions may be "outside" of departmental norms but are often extremely valuable.

Finally, this free-response activity may be useful to TAs in the classroom. For instance, during recitations TAs can distribute cards and ask students to write down one topic, item, or concept that was most interesting or most confusing in the previous lecture or reading; they can ask students to write down how a specific concept could be explained to non-concentrator friends. Alternatively, this technique can be used at the end of a class, and students can be asked to write down what they found most confusing or interesting about the class that day. Although this is a standard technique, some TAs may not be familiar with it. Giving TAs the opportunity to experience the technique themselves may help them to envision its implementation into their own classrooms. It is helpful if this logic is explained to the group as part of the TA training. In addition, as part of the training, the facilitator can ask participants to share ways in which they might utilize this free-response technique in their courses.

An Approach to Successful Collaborative Learning

Nancy C. McClure

Fairmont State University

GOALS

- To demonstrate a Jigsaw activity—a collaborative learning technique that requires each student to contribute to the learning process
- To introduce TAs to the Jigsaw approach through involvement in the process

PREPARATION TIME

15–30 minutes for gathering resources prior to session

EXECUTION TIME

45–60 minutes

ASSUMPTIONS

For the example provided, there are 35 TAs attending the training. However, any material can be used, and the groups adjust accordingly.

RESOURCES

One copy of the web resource "Seven Principles for Good Practice in Undergraduate Education" by Chickering and Gamson (www.fctel.uncc.edu/pedagogy/enhancinglearning/SevenPrinciples.html)

Introduction

Managing groups presents a challenge for most teachers, but those who possess a repertoire of strategies approach group work more confidently than those who don't. The Jigsaw approach offers TAs a proven method for organizing groups and keeping undergraduates on task. The process involves putting students in base groups and then giving each student in each base group a part of the assignment for which he or she is responsible. Students from each base group who have the same part of the assignment meet in expert groups to learn their part and prepare to teach it to their base groups. The experts then go back to their base groups, where everyone shares his or her part of the whole—thus, the experts put the "pieces" of the "jigsaw puzzle" into place.

The number of base group members depends on the number of pieces there are to the assignment. For example, if there are seven pieces to learn, then there are seven people in the group (see the following example). If the class is smaller, have students become experts for more than one piece of the puzzle.

Procedure

1. Provide each TA with a copy of Chickering and Gamson's "Seven Principles for Good Practice in Undergraduate Education."

2. Form five groups of seven TAs each. These are the base groups. Assign a different principle to each of the seven members of each group.

3. Have students move into their expert groups. That is, everyone who has Principle 1 will work together, everyone who has Principle 2 will work together, and so on.

4. Each group discusses and learns the principle you have assigned. They also decide how they will teach it. Each member of the expert group will be responsible for teaching the material to his or her own base group.

5. At the end of the allotted time, have TAs return to their base groups.

6. Each member of the base group explains his or her principle to the rest of the group. In this manner, each of the seven principles is covered in each group.

Blended Learning: Focusing on Effective Teaching Through Online Discussions and Concept Mapping

Gabriele Bauer

University of Delaware

GOALS
- To teach TAs how to construct a concept map using guided online discussions
- To enable TAs to apply concept mapping to their own teaching contexts

CONTEXT
- Blended learning environment: The course/seminar series combines aspects of online and face-to-face instruction.
- Part of the course is delivered via a course management system, WebCT or Blackboard.

PREPARATION TIME
- Posting of online discussion questions prior to class
- 10-minute overview and examples of concept maps (graphic organizers) in class

EXECUTION TIME
45–60 minutes in class

RESOURCES
- List of items generated via online discussion
- Post-it notes
- Self-stick easel pad and pens

Introduction

An online discussion posting gives students the opportunity to assess their prior understanding of a common instructional topic, share this understanding with their peers, receive feedback, and integrate alternative understandings with their own. Online discussion provides an anonymous setting for in-depth discussion and exploration of peers' thinking that leads directly to further analysis and synthesis of the material in class.

Procedure

Before Class

1. The instructor posts a series of open-ended questions for online discussion, such as: What does it mean to be an effective instructor in

your discipline? How would you know an effective instructor if you saw one? What are characteristics of effective teaching in your field? From a faculty perspective? From a student perspective? From an administrative perspective?

2. Students post to the online discussion, respond to one another's postings, and provide concrete examples. The instructor listens in, probes, questions, challenges, and offers resources.

3. Two students are asked to review the postings; look for examples, descriptions, terms, and ideas that are associated with the topic; and make a list of these items in preparation for the in-class meeting.

In Class

1. The instructor provides an overview of concept mapping and its instructional purpose and shows examples. This is followed by clarification and questions.

2. Students get into cross-disciplinary groups (four to five members). Each group uses the list generated via the online discussion as a starting point for portraying their group-based understanding of effective teaching.

3. Students print the items on post-it notes, one per note, in a brief form (e.g., single word or short phrase). The group can add items to the list.

4. Students organize items, introduce new items that they omitted initially to create groups and subgroups of related items.

5. On a large sheet of paper, students determine a layout that best represents their collective understanding of the connections among groupings. They transition from a practice-based (experiential) level to a conceptual (theoretical) level.

6. Students title their concept maps, sign them, and display them around the room. They review the maps from other groups and note similarities, observations, and questions.

7. Each group presents two to three main points from their concept maps and answers questions as appropriate.

8. This is followed by a class discussion that incorporates readings and research on effective teaching.

Variations

1. Conduct this group concept-mapping activity as an end-of-course summary to assess student learning. This allows for a pre- and post-comparison of the level of understanding and improved skill in concept map construction. It also communicates to student groups progression in their learning.

2. Bring concept maps back to the course at appropriate times so that groups can incorporate new content learned and revisit accuracy, completeness, and organization. This serves as a parameter of how student understanding of a topic develops and expands.

Diversity in the Classroom: Working Effectively with Undergraduate ESL Students

Shawna Shapiro
University of Washington

GOALS
- To offer an overview of the strengths and needs of nonnative English speakers
- To share effective instructional strategies that account for these factors

PREPARATION TIME
Depends on experience

EXECUTION TIME
60–75 minutes, depending on the context and number of participants

RESOURCES
None

Introduction

The continued growth of international and immigrant student populations in most colleges and universities has led to more linguistically and culturally diverse classrooms nationwide. Yet many instructors feel they lack the knowledge and skills needed to understand, support, and enhance the learning process for these multilingual students. This two-part workshop provides information and pedagogical techniques that have proven effective. Part I presents general information and guidelines to inform instructors about this population of students. Part II demonstrates the application of this information in various elements of classroom instruction: lecture and presentation, discussion and participation, assignments and assessment, and conferencing. These two parts are integrated throughout the workshop, enabling students to gain both general insights and specific strategies.

Procedure

1. Students form small groups to discuss three opening questions:
   - What is your current or anticipated teaching situation?
   - What do you know thus far about the experiences, characteristics, and/or needs of nonnative speakers of English?
   - What would you like to learn from this workshop?

2. Follow-up: The presenter discusses responses to the first question and explains that the rest of the workshop will expand on the second question as well as fulfill the third question.

3. The presenter distributes Table 1.1 and explains how it will be used. This is followed by discussion of general implications for instruction.

4. The presenter introduces Table 1.2 (highlighting some points) and then solicits "application" responses from participants in small groups, each focusing on generating questions, details, and examples for a particular column of the chart.

5. Follow-up: The presenter revisits the first and third questions from the opening discussion to determine if other points or questions should be addressed.

Variations

1. Part I can also be done as a "carousel brainstorm," where students mill about the classroom and fill in answers (on butcher paper or poster board).

2. If time allows, the group may wish to analyze the workshop itself, examining the ways in which the presenter attempted to follow the guidelines. (In other words, asking "How well did this workshop follow its own suggestions for effective instruction?")

TABLE 1.1 • **WHO ARE ESL STUDENTS?**

	International Students ("Eye" learners)	**Immigrant Students** ("Ear" learners)
Educational Background	• Global context • Traditional instruction (usually) • Academic English • Higher socioeconomic status (often, but not always)	• More experience in the United States • High school in the United States (may have taken ESL courses) • Communicative English often stronger than academic English
Strengths	• Reading • Grammar knowledge • Motivation and objectives • Academic skills (overall) • Responsiveness to instructor	• Speaking and listening • Cultural knowledge • Support system (family, friends) • Responsiveness to instructor
Challenges and Needs (Linguistic, cultural, academic, personal)	• Grammar application • Speaking and listening • Appropriateness in vocabulary • Cultural adjustment (often lack support system) • U.S. academic culture • Asking for help	• Academic literacy • Academic vocabulary • College preparedness (critical thinking, metacognition) • Cultural identity (sense of between-ness) • Confidence in academic skill • Asking for help

TABLE 1.2 • **HOW CAN I BEST SUPPORT ESL STUDENTS?**

General Guidelines	Lecture/ Presentation Ideas	Discussion and Group Work Ideas	Assignments and Assessment Ideas
Inform yourself about students and elicit regular feedback	• Large group short-response questions • Three-minute "reflection" from students on what they've learned (or what they know beforehand)	• Encourage written participation, not just speaking. • Hold a small group discussion with written report handed in to you. (Small group activities work particularly well with "eye" learners who need more processing time.)	• Use surveys, questionnaires, and the like to learn more about students. • Student reflections (e.g., "writers' memo" attached to an assignment) • Low-stakes quizzes and other small assessments are preferable to large exams.
Vary modes of instruction	• Elicit kinesthetic feedback (raise hands, stand) to check for understanding. • Present information in multiple ways (say it, write it, model it). • Use the Internet to find helpful materials and links. (If it's being taught, someone has probably posted useful information on the web and hopes you or your students will use it.)	• Ask both open-ended and limited-response questions. • Encourage students to share from their cultural backgrounds (e.g., How might this issue or problem have been perceived or addressed in other countries?). • Vary group sizes (two to five students).	• Possible alternative assignment genres: poster, pamphlet/ brochure, book cover, letter to editor (or to mom), chart/graphic, creative writing (poem, story, fictional letter, dialogue), movie design, interview • Use review games and activities, and/or help students form study groups. • Have students "re-teach" a partner, to review and check for understanding.

General Guidelines	Lecture/ Presentation Ideas	Discussion and Group Work Ideas	Assignments and Assessment Ideas
Be as visual and explicit as possible	• Highlight unfamiliar concepts and vocabulary before using them in lecture. • Include examples and applications of abstract concepts. • Visual aids: charts, graphs, examples, pictures, note-taking grids	• Provide focused questions for discussion (in large and small groups). • Designate roles within groups (note-taker, presenter, timekeeper, task manager, etc.). • Ask groups of students to come up with new examples, applications, or visual aids for a concept.	• Offer clear grading criteria: models, guidelines, rubrics, illustrations. • Comment selectively and specifically on student work (quality vs. quantity in your feedback). • If you choose to "mark" grammar errors, limit yourself to a couple of pages, since the same errors will be repeated.
Give options when possible (but avoid too many options)	• Consider offering an optional "workshop" for struggling students. • Provide time for student questions before lecture (make it HW?).	• Offer a written (electronic) discussion board as a continuation of class time. • Consider forming teacher-assigned groups (to mix things occasionally).	• Opportunities for rewrite or other revision of work (test corrections for partial credit) • Limit the number of options given (for your sake and theirs).
Know your resources	Writing center web sites, departmental colleagues, other campus groups focused on teaching		

Engaging Students in Active Learning

Shawna Shapiro
University of Washington

GOALS
- To offer a rationale and framework for incorporating active learning into university-level courses
- To provide examples of activities that can be used across disciplines

PREPARATION TIME
Depends on experience

EXECUTION TIME
60–75 minutes, depending on the context and number of participants

RESOURCES
None

Introduction

University-level instructors often assume that active learning is impossible in postsecondary settings. Yet this belief ignores research on the learning processes and brain development of students—research that shows that both short-term learning and long-term retention are enhanced by instruction that actively engages students. This workshop aims to broaden the definition of *active learning* by offering both general guidelines and specific examples for instructors wishing to increase their students' engagement in learning.

Procedure

1. Students form small groups and discuss the following questions:
   - How would you describe active learning?
   - What is one memory you have of being an actively engaged student?
   - What did that instructor do to help you engage in learning?
2. Small groups report back to the large group. The instructor facilitates discussion, pointing out similarities or differences from among the descriptions and examples.
3. The instructor presents four guidelines (following this activity) for active learning instruction, discusses each one, and asks for questions or examples.

4. The instructor discusses and demonstrates many of the ideas in the list, including asking workshop attendees to stand, based on their preferences as learners. (I call this a "body survey": Stand if you like playing games in classes. Stand if you like puzzles and problem-solving exercises.)

Variations

1. The first procedure could be completed more kinesthetically by having participants mill about the classroom, writing answers on butcher paper or a whiteboard.

2. Students could participate in a meta-discussion about their own level of engagement in the workshop itself and the elements that contributed to this engagement.

3. The instructor may wish to use a game or other activity to review or reinforce what has been covered in the workshop.

Guidelines for Active Learning

Variety: The "Spice" of the Classroom

- Using a variety of activities, groupings, and presentation methods increases student engagement. But like any spice, it is possible to go overboard.

Remember that Unexpected = Interesting

- Use the element of surprise to heighten engagement.

Be Aware that Multisensory = More Active

- Most students are more visual than auditory. (Almost all students remember more what they *experience* through their 5+ senses.)
- Active learning does not need to be elaborate, expensive, or incredibly entertaining. Some simple additions and modifications to traditional pedagogy can make a world of difference.

Don't Try to Please Everyone

- Students have various preferences, learning styles, and attitudes (especially early in the morning). You'll almost always have one or two who would rather sleep than engage in learning.

Techniques for Fostering Active Learning

Lecture/Presentation

- Elicit feedback through *physical response* (standing, raising hand, moving around room).
- *Inductive* versus deductive presentation (start with the end point and work backwards; move from concrete application and examples toward more abstract principles)
- Use *pictures, cartoons, photographs, and scenarios* to get thoughts going.
- *Jigsaw:* Have students prepare sections to present in small groups or to the entire class.

Participation and Discussion

- Pass around a (squishy) *ball* or have students call on the next person to answer a question. This keeps students engaged and levels the playing field for participation.
- Draw names from *cards,* rather than calling on students.
- Use *multiple groupings* (e.g., Think-Pair-Share).
- *Carousel sharing* (have students write responses on butcher paper or transparency)
- *Debate* (with moderators, to ensure participation from both sides and many participants)
- *Fishbowl questions* (students draw from a "hat" to answer in front of the class)
- In-class *research and report* (students survey each other and present their findings to the class)

Review/Assessment

- *Review (or assessment!) games:* Jeopardy, $10,000 Pyramid (AKA "Password"), Around the World, Find Your Match (dating game), Outburst (categories), Pictionary, Charades, Who Am I?, Board Races, Reading Relay, Trashketball
- *Student-designed games or quiz questions* (It's amazing what they come up with, and this saves you time!)

- *Variety in assignments:* poster, pamphlet/brochure, book cover, letter to editor (or to mom), chart or graphic, creative writing (poem, story, fictional letter, dialogue), movie design, interview

General/Miscellaneous

- *First day/week:* Bingo/Find Someone Who . . ., Fruit Basket, silent conversation
- *Motivators:* prizes (including coupons), extra credit or privileges (leaving early), common class goal (party, field trip, etc.)

Identity and Authority in the Classroom: An Exercise for New TAs

Mary C. Wright
University of Michigan

GOALS

- To allow new TAs to think through how their identities may affect classroom dynamics
- To proactively prepare classroom strategies in line with these dynamics

PREPARATION TIME

Minimal

EXECUTION TIME

30 minutes

RESOURCES

- "Guidelines for Class Participation" from the Center for Research on Learning and Teaching's *Graduate Student Instructor Guidebook* (www.crlt.umich.edu/gsis/P4_1.html)
- Social Characteristics handout (following this activity)
- "Constructing and Maintaining Authority in Inclusive Classrooms" by A. T. Miller from the Center for Research on Learning and Teaching's *Graduate Student Instructor Guidebook* (www.crlt.umich.edu/gsis/P4_2.html)
- "Dealing with Troublesome Behaviors in the Classroom" by Sorcinelli (1994)

Introduction

Many new TAs are concerned about developing and maintaining authority in the classroom. However, the means by which TAs can develop these strategies will differ because of their own identities (e.g., age, race, gender, nationality) and often in ways they do not anticipate. This activity allows TAs to think through characteristics of their social identity that might be salient in their teaching before they enter the classroom for the first time. New TAs are then able to develop pedagogical strategies to create the type of classroom atmosphere they wish to develop. It also models how to navigate discussions of difficult topics.

Procedure

Part I: Preparation for Exercise (5 minutes)

1. Show participants an example of classroom guidelines (e.g., "Guidelines for class participation"). Specify that these guidelines lay

the foundation for basic respect among students—and also between students and the TA. Note that there may be certain contexts where it's inappropriate to use guidelines, but in many cases—even when the course content at first seems to not suggest it—they are useful (e.g., a statistics class where some word problems or interpretations of analyses could raise a heated discussion).

2. Next, the group will discuss identity issues, which can become complicated. Tell participants that you are going to use these guidelines for the discussion that follows. Ask participants if they have any suggestions for additions or modifications to the list. If there are any, write them on a board or easel.

Part II: Exercise and Debrief (25 minutes)

1. Pass out the "Social Characteristics" handout (following this activity).
   - First, ask participants to fill out the "How do you identify?" column. Point out that there is an "other" row for those parts of their identity that they feel are important to who they are but aren't listed on the page.
   - Second, ask participants to move to the next column: "Check the boxes where you feel others see you differently than you see yourself." An example is often useful here (e.g., you identify as Afro-Caribbean but people see you as African-American).
   - Third, ask participants to move to the next column: "On the first day of class, how will students see you? Check the characteristics that you think are most likely to form their initial perception of you."
   - Fourth, ask participants to move to the last column: "What other characteristics might you want to disclose or discuss openly in class?" Explain that this decision could be influenced by subject matter.

2. In small groups, have participants discuss the questions on the handout: How might student reactions to these characteristics be an asset for you as you teach? A challenge? What strategies can you use if a challenge arises?

3. Quickly debrief, collecting some ideas of strategies. "Constructing and Maintaining Authority in Inclusive Classrooms" and Sorcinelli (1994) serve as useful resources for other strategies.

Variations

Questions in the columns can be modified as needed.

Acknowledgments

This activity was designed with assistance from the Center for Research on Learning and Teaching Graduate Student Instructor team: Crisca Bierwert, Chad Hershock, Matt Kaplan, and Tershia Pinder.

References

Sorcinelli, M. D. (1994). Dealing with troublesome behaviors in the classroom. In K. W. Prichard & R. M. Sawyer (Eds.), *Handbook of college teaching: Theory and applications* (pp. 365–373). Westport, CT: Greenwood Press.

Social Characteristics

Social Characteristics	1. How do you identify?	2. Others see you differently?	3. How students see you?	4. Others to disclose?
Race/ethnicity				
Gender				
Class				
Physical ability				
Sexual orientation				
Religion				
Age				
Other salient characteristics				

Debrief Questions

- How might student reactions to these characteristics be an asset for you as you teach? A challenge?
- What strategies can you use if a challenge arises?

Adapted from Social Group Membership Profile (NPI) and Professor Mark Chesler, University of Michigan.

Planning and Facilitating Discussion

Phillip M. Edwards, Stacy Grooters, Margaret Lawrence

University of Washington

GOALS

By the end of this workshop, participants should be able to:

- Identify when discussion is a good choice for meeting student learning objectives.
- Prepare themselves and their students for an effective in-class discussion.
- Utilize techniques for facilitating effective discussions and encouraging participation.
- Anticipate possible trouble spots and employ strategies for addressing them.

PREPARATION TIME

For workshop leaders, a minimum of 1 to 2 hours to assemble any necessary resources, depending largely on the experience of the leader and availability of materials. For workshop participants, no previous preparation is necessary.

EXECUTION TIME

75 minutes

RESOURCES

If following the specific plan described here, you may need to locate a quote related to teaching and learning to use for developing a common frame of reference among workshop participants. You may provide this to each participant on a handout, or you could display it on overhead or write it on the board.

Introduction

Throughout this workshop, it is as important to model and reflect on strategies for facilitating a discussion as it is to talk about what makes a good discussion. Therefore, you may want to periodically have the group step back and have a meta-discussion about the workshop. For instance, you can ask participants to consider their own participation in classes as a student: When were they most likely to participate? When did they hold back? How can being aware of these factors make them better discussion facilitators? How do they react to silences or breaks in the discussion? In thinking about incorporating opportunities for meta-discussion, you may find that topics difficult to model directly (e.g., the planning process behind the workshop) become easier to engage when you and the participants reflect on the common experiences of being workshop participants. In addition, the individual leading this workshop should be comfortable with a variety of techniques for facilitating discussion: providing mechanisms for tracking the discussion, redirecting questions back to participants, resisting the temptation to respond to every comment, and being comfortable with silence. The Planning and Facilitating Discussion workshop explores strategies for initiating, maintaining, tracking, and concluding class discussions by modeling these techniques for participants, then asking participants to reflect on each technique's effectiveness.

Procedure

Stage 1 (15–20 minutes)

1. Prior to the arrival of participants, arrange the chairs in a circle or similar physical arrangement that allows you to sit among the participants or along the periphery of the group.

2. At the beginning of the workshop, have each participant share a brief personal introduction with the group. This can be a good time to find out the kinds of experiences your group of TAs has had with classroom discussion, how those experiences impact the way they approach discussions, how disciplinary differences affect why/how they incorporate discussion into class, and any anxieties they have about leading a discussion.

3. Introduce a common frame of reference for the session. This might be a quote related to teaching and learning in higher education, life as a graduate student, or a similar general sentiment that speaks broadly to the participants' experiences or anxieties. For example, one of the contributors [PME] uses the following quote:

> I had finally realized that what I was actually concerned with and focused on most of the time were three things: a) to show the students how smart I was, b) to show them how knowledgeable I was, and c) to show them how well-prepared I was for class. . . . Fear is the driving force behind the performance model. Fear of being shown up for what you are: a fraud, stupid, ignorant, a clod, a dolt, a sap, a weakling, someone who can't cut the mustard. (Tompkins, 1990, p. 654)

Because this quote displays both hyperbole related to the author's self-perceptions and a very real vulnerability, participants sharing this anxiety seem reassured to hear that this sentiment has been expressed in a public forum. You may find it helpful to leverage these visceral responses as a transition into talking about discussion.

(One possible transition: "How many of you can identify with this anxiety? Perhaps this anxiety is most pronounced among new instructors when dealing with discussion in their classrooms. Let's spend some time talking together about class discussion . . .")

Stage 2 (40–45 minutes)

1. Have participants free-write for one to two minutes in response to one of the following prompts: "Discussion can accomplish . . . ," "One of the goals of discussion is . . . ," or "Classroom discussion helps students . . ."

2. Once everyone seems to have written something, have each participant talk about what they've written with one or two of their nearby peers.

3. After all groups have interacted, have them report their responses to the large group. Write these contributions on the board as a means of tracking the discussion and encourage students to think about how these goals might be approached in each participant's discipline. (Alternatively, you may ask for a volunteer to record these contributions to preserve your image as the facilitator on the periphery of the discussion.) This may also be an excellent opportunity to entertain suggestions about when discussion might not be an ideal instructional method in particular contexts.

4. Once the list of responses to the prompt about goals/benefits appears complete, provide a second prompt: "What are barriers to these goals or challenges that might get in the way?" In the interest of varying classroom activities, you may consider having the large group respond to this prompt without another free-write/Think-Pair-Share activity. You or a volunteer scribe could write these suggestions on the board.

5. Once the list of responses to the prompt about challenges is complete, provide a third prompt: "What are some ways of addressing these challenges?" Again, you or a volunteer scribe could note these suggestions on the board.

Stage 3 (10–15 minutes)

1. With approximately 10–15 minutes remaining in the session, have participants refocus their attention on the complete list of goals/benefits, challenges, and techniques that have been noted during the discussion.

2. Provide the following prompt: "In thinking about the discussions of the past hour, do you recall seeing any of these benefits, challenges, or techniques taking place?"
   - Ask students to think about the characteristics of the prompts used during the session or the use of the icebreaker activity (i.e., the quote about teaching) as an introduction for the discussion.
   - Highlight the items that students recall on the board. Make sure to allow all participants adequate time to transcribe notes from this list before they leave the workshop.
   - If you are concerned about participants leaving without concrete examples to apply in their teaching, you may suggest that participants write down one or two examples of strategies or techniques that seem most useful or that they would like to explore further.

References

Tompkins, J. (1990, October). Pedagogy of the distressed. *College English, 52*(6), 653–660.

Problems, Pitfalls, and Surprises in Teaching: Mini Cases

Lori Breslow, J. Mark Schuster
Massachusetts Institute of Technology

GOALS
To give TAs an opportunity to brainstorm how they would handle potential challenges that can arise inside and outside the classroom

PREPARATION TIME
None

EXECUTION TIME
Variable, depending on how many cases are discussed; allow 15–20 minutes per case

RESOURCES
Mini cases (examples provided), guidelines following this activity

Introduction

All teachers are challenged at one time or another by difficult situations or by a problem with a particular student. These problems can range from getting students to participate in class, to the student who talks too much, to problems related to cultural diversity or gender. TAs may also need to help students with personal problems or to deal with cases of plagiarism or cheating. In addition, the interaction between the TA and the faculty member who is providing the course lectures can sometimes be difficult. The scenarios discussed here describe some of these dilemmas. They are similar in that none of them has a right or wrong answer. Instead there are a variety of approaches that may be successful, and this exercise gives TAs an opportunity to think through the possibilities.

Procedure

1. Have one student read the scenario out loud. Ask the group for questions about any aspect of the situation that is to be discussed. (2 minutes)

2. Arrange students in pairs or in small groups and allow them to brainstorm possible ways of handing the situation. (7–10 minutes)

3. Return students to the larger group and debrief the small group discussions. (10–12 minutes)

After students have reviewed several scenarios, it is helpful to provide a synthesis of the best practices that have been discussed during the session. Some of the points often highlighted include:

- Resources at your university to help you with your problem. Those resources can include faculty in the department, counselors, physicians, and a teaching and learning center.
- Ways that a difficult situation might be turned into an opportunity for learning.
- The fact that each student is a member of the larger group that comprises the class as a whole. Keep issues of fairness in mind.
- Honesty as the best policy.
- That you must listen carefully to make sure you have all necessary information before making a decision.
- Teachers as human beings. Admit to and share your humanity.

Here are six sample scenarios:

1. You have a student in class who always has a hand raised to answer questions you have asked. Soon it seems other students in your recitation don't raise their hands because they know this student will have the answer. What do you do?

2. You have a student you feel is constantly challenging you in front of the other students: He always asks questions in a tone you feel subtly undermines your authority. What do you do?

3. A student comes to you after receiving her graded homework (or her midterm, her final exam, her course grade). She is very angry about the grade, feeling that it does not reflect her command of the material. What do you do?

4. You do not want students to have their laptops open or their cell phones on when in class. How do you communicate this requirement? Include it in the syllabus? Announce it on the first day of class? Assume you don't say anything at the beginning of the semester, but discover students are surfing the web, text messaging, and so on during class. It's now three weeks into the semester. What do you do?

5. Two of the students in your class handed in identical solutions for the last homework assignment. The only difference was their names in the upper corner. What should you do? Would your reaction be

different if this happened on the midterm exam? In a related context, you are reading one of your student's final papers and begin to feel uneasy because it does not seem to be written in the student's own voice. You go to the library (or to various web sites) to check his references and discover that major portions of the paper have been copied from these references, sometimes with some paraphrasing, sometimes word for word. What should you do?

6. No matter what you try, you find it nearly impossible to get students to participate in classroom discussions. They almost never contribute; they hardly ever ask questions; they offer answers to your questions only reluctantly. What can you do?

Variations

If short on time, assign pairs of students different scenarios and ask them to report back to the larger group.

Handling Problems, Pitfalls, and Surprises in Teaching: Some Guidelines

In workshops, suggestions about how to handle the problems in the scenarios under discussion have surfaced. Those ideas have been distilled into some guidelines to help you handle many of the challenges that will arise in your teaching career. These guidelines fall into several broad categories.

1. **Be aware that two kinds of contracts exist in the classroom.**
   Two kinds of contracts govern the expectations and behavior of both instructor and students in any classroom: 1) the *explicit contract,* which is often spelled out in the syllabus and covers such aspects of the course as weekly classroom topics, course requirements, and course expectations; and 2) the *implicit contract,* which stipulates norms such as who can talk in the classroom, what styles of teaching are used, and what styles of learning are emphasized. Give careful thought to the explicit contract; it is directly in your control, particularly at the outset of the semester. But also be conscious of the implicit contract, particularly as it evolves through precedent in the classroom interactions of your course. Monitor it and respect it throughout the semester.

2. **You are a human being. Admit to and share your humanity.**
   This guideline is, perhaps, a corollary of the previous one. You can make your teaching life a very complicated one if you think teaching is neither nothing more nor nothing less than delivering information. What seems critical is to figure out how to be yourself through your teaching. Then you will accept the role of teacher easily and comfortably, and honesty will be easy to accomplish. Students see through artificial poses, as they should. Be yourself.

3. **Use outside resources, including colleagues. Remember, you are not alone.**
   Your university has resources available to help with difficult situations that arise in the classroom. That you have been asked to teach is not, in itself, a validation sticker on your teaching abilities. Teaching skills can be developed and honed, and your university provides a lot of resources to help you in that growth. These may range from an ombudsmen to written policies on cheating and plagiarism to a guide on handling sexual harassment. One of the most

valuable resources at your disposal consists of fellow faculty members and fellow TAs. Use colleagues as sounding boards as you develop your own teaching style and as you work your way through some of the problems that will inevitably challenge you.

4. **Honesty is the best policy.**

   We have experienced very few issues in education that are not addressed best with honesty. If you do not know the answer to a student's question, admit it, but promise to find the answer before the next meeting. If you find yourself in a dilemma to which there is no ideal solution, say so. Provide a truthful reason for why a policy is what it is, and if you do not understand why it is what it is, say so, but once again promise to find out.

5. **Listen with empathy and make sure you have all necessary information before making a decision.**

   Listen intelligently and carefully to a student when he or she comes to talk to you about a problem. Try to sidestep any preconceived notions about the student, the problem, the class as a whole, and so on. Put yourself into his or her shoes and attempt to determine both the *meaning* and *feeling* behind what the student is saying. Recognize those feelings (e.g., "It must feel terrible that . . ."). Make sure you talk to all concerned parties before deciding on a course of action, and remember that the issue that is under discussion may not be the underlying problem.

6. **Think strategically about the problem.**

   By *strategic* thinking we mean analyze the problem you have been confronted with by answering the following questions:

   - *What is my purpose in this situation?* Every problem or difficulty represents an opportunity to accomplish one or more teaching goals. Can this situation provide a chance for learning? Can you use this problem to change the learning environment in the classroom? To the extent that you can determine beforehand what you want to achieve, you will be able to decide on an appropriate response more effectively.
   - *What are the characteristics of the students who are involved in this situation?* Knowing something about the personalities and backgrounds of your students will help guide your response. For example, the norms in some cultures dictate that students should be silent in the classroom, neither participating in class discussions

nor asking questions. This norm might account for the unusually quiet behavior of some students, and that knowledge could help you aid those students in modifying their style of expression.

- *What responses and/or feelings are brought up in me as a result of this situation? How can I use my particular teaching style and communication skills most effectively?* It is not unusual that teaching dilemmas bring up strong feelings in the instructor. For example, you may feel uncomfortable addressing gender issues in the classroom or trying to communicate with a student who is a nonnative English speaker. Recognizing these feelings in yourself will help you frame an effective response. Similarly, we all come with teaching and communication strengths that we can call on to help us cope with difficult situations. A sense of humor, the power to observe closely, or the ability to work at different levels of abstraction may all be used to handle effectively the kinds of pitfalls we have been discussing.
- *What medium would be the most effective to use in this situation?* Is this a situation that is best handled by a meeting with the student? By writing a memo or letter? By addressing the issue with the class as a whole? Each strategy has its own benefits and liabilities, and sometimes using a combination of media is best.
- *What cultural variables are affecting the situation?* Cultural variables are at work in the classroom on several different levels. Every course and classroom has its own climate, every university has its own distinct culture, and your students bring the norms of their home countries and/or of their peer groups into the classroom. Recognizing this diversity of norms will help you understand their impact on the situation and respond accordingly.

7. **Think about ways a difficult situation might be turned into a learning opportunity.**
All kinds of learning take place in the classroom in addition to mastering a certain subject area. Students are learning how to learn, how to work with others, how scholars in the field think, and so on. Often difficulties in the classroom can be used as vehicles that contribute to these kinds of learning.

8. **Remember that each student is a member of the larger group that comprises the class as a whole. Keep issues of fairness in mind.**
Often the thorniest dilemmas in teaching involve balancing the needs of the individual student with the needs and rights of the class as a

whole. To use the quiet student as an example again, if a student is from a culture where silence in the classroom is a norm, should that student be penalized for not contributing to classroom discussion? On the other hand, is it fair to have two sets of standards in one classroom? And are other students in the class missing valuable contributions because the expectation of particular modes of classroom behavior impedes the ability of some students to speak in public?

Another challenging situation is that of the monopolizing student. Students talk too much for a variety of reasons, including genuine excitement about a topic, insensitivity, nerves, and problems with impulse control. Generally, a good approach to dealing with both the excessively talkative or quiet student is to meet one-on-one outside class to talk and establish strategies to ameliorate the situation.

Similarly, recognize that once a student has asked a question (raised an issue, or expressed a viewpoint), that question may then become the question of other members of the class, and it may no longer be sufficient to respond to that individual student alone.

These suggestions are not meant to be inclusive. Instead, they are an attempt to help TAs think through ways to handle the problems, pitfalls, and surprises they will face in their teaching careers. We hope these guidelines will provide a springboard to an ongoing conversation about teaching in higher education.

Responding to Student Writing

Stacy Grooters, Jennie Dorman

University of Washington

GOALS

By the end of this workshop, participants should be able to:

- Evaluate an assignment's goals in order to plan an effective response strategy.
- Distinguish between "writing to learn" and "writing to demonstrate learning" assignments.
- Begin to construct a basic rubric for evaluating student writing.

PREPARATION TIME

For workshop leaders, a minimum of 1 to 2 hours to assemble any necessary resources, depending largely on the leader's previous experience and the availability of materials. For workshop participants, no previous preparation is necessary.

EXECUTION TIME

75 minutes

RESOURCES

Copies of various writing assignments, rubrics, and sample student papers from a single discipline or from a variety of fields

Introduction

The audience for the workshop described here ranges in size from 20–35 participants from a wide variety of disciplinary backgrounds, over half of whom have had less than one year of formal teaching experience. The Responding to Student Writing workshop explores different strategies for reading and responding to student writing; it focuses less on specific grading techniques and more on crafting response strategies that are tailored to address a particular assignment.

Procedure

Stage 1 (10–15 minutes)

1. Drawing on TAs' experiences to set the stage: Options for the first 10–15 minutes. TAs often appreciate a chance to talk about their worries or fears about responding to student writing. Have participants free-write for a short time and then discuss in small groups (about 15 minutes) based on one or more of these prompts:

- What is one problem you have had when giving students feedback on their writing?
- What concerns do you fear will arise when giving students feedback on their writing?
- What different kinds of feedback have you received on your writing, and what properties of this feedback either made it helpful or scarred you forever?

2. Briefly follow-up with the groups, listing their main concerns on the board. Refer back to these concerns, as appropriate, throughout the workshop. Note: When talking about "writing to learn" or low-stakes assignments later in the workshop, you might refer back to this initial free-write as an example of how one can incorporate a low-stakes writing assignment into a class that does not necessarily need a lot of in-depth response (or any response at all) from the instructor.

3. As a lead-in for talking about high-stakes/low-stakes assignments, get TAs to think about the different learning purposes served by different kinds of writing assignments. This activity encourages TAs to consider gearing their response strategies to address the goals of an assignment, rather than just responding to all assignments in the same way. Have TAs work individually or in small groups to:
- Brainstorm a list of all the different kinds of writing assignments they have encountered, both as in-class and take-home assignments.
- Have them choose a few and discuss the purpose of those assignments (e.g., what were the instructor's goals in assigning it?).
- Ask them to consider if they would respond differently to those assignments based on the goals they address. Highlight the differences in how they would respond to high- and low-stakes (or "writing to learn" and "writing to demonstrate learning") assignments.

Variation for step 3. An alternative would be to facilitate a brainstorming session in which the participants list all the reasons they can think of for responding to student writing. Then draw attention to how these tend to fall into categories of responding to 1) in-process writing and 2) finished writing (thus getting them ready for talking about high- or low-stakes writing). Some possible reasons TAs might list include to give feedback for revision, to prepare students for later assignments/exams, to provide encouragement, to offer a different perspective, to acknowledge completed work; to explain a grade, to help students learn.

Stage 2 (40–45 minutes)

1. Discuss the difference between high- and low-stakes assignments. See Peter Elbow and Mary Deane Sorcinelli's chapter "How to Enhance Learning by Using High-Stakes and Low-Stakes Writing" in the 12th edition of *McKeachie's Teaching Tips* (2006).

2. Have the participants work in groups to evaluate one or two sample assignments in order to plan how they would respond to papers written for the assignments. You can ask them to consider questions such as:
   - What is the purpose of the assignment?
   - Is the assignment high or low stakes?
   - How will the students use your comments?
   - What will students want to know from you?
   - What would you choose not to comment on?

   Variation for step 2. Collect an assortment of different rubrics, divide the participants into groups, and then have each group look through a set of rubrics to identify the strengths and weaknesses. It might also be helpful to ask participants to group the rubrics according to assignment purpose, discipline, and so forth, and note the differences. You could also give groups of participants a simple assignment example asking them to begin delineating what categories they would focus on, how they would weigh those categories, and how they would organize them into a rubric. Encourage participants to use the sample rubrics for ideas.

Stage 3 (15–20 minutes)

1. Have TAs practice responding to a student paper:
   - Give TAs some context for the paper—for example, let them read the assignment description, explain where it comes during the term, make sure the goals of the assignment are clear.
   - Ask them to talk in groups about how they intend to respond to the paper.
   - Give them time individually to respond to the paper.
   - Ask them to talk again about how well their strategies worked.

2. You may want to consider the following issues as well:
   - Try to include the assignment description with the paper so participants can see what purpose the assignment had. You might choose to use the same assignment that you evaluated earlier in talking about low-stakes assignments or rubrics.
   - Keep the paper short enough so that participants don't feel rushed.

References

Elbow, P., & Sorcinelli, M. D. (2006). How to enhance learning by using high-stakes and low-stakes writing. In W. J. McKeachie & M. Svinicki, *McKeachie's Teaching Tips* (12th ed., pp. 192–212). Boston, MA: Houghton Mifflin.

Stand and Deliver: Developing Impromptu Speaking Skills

Jane Dunphy
Massachusetts Institute of Technology

GOALS

To demystify spontaneous speaking by providing guidelines and practice

PREPARATION TIME

20 minutes to introduce the activity

EXECUTION TIME

1–2 minutes per impromptu; 1–2 minutes of feedback (5–10 minutes per class period over a semester; or 45 minutes on each day of a multiday orientation)

ASSUMPTIONS

Participants are familiar with a variety of "gambits" (conventional phrases in spoken English) for such speech acts as hesitating, buying time, organizing information, stating opinions, and providing feedback.

RESOURCES

List of suitable topics (following this activity)

Introduction

Speaking with little advance preparation can be intimidating, yet effective impromptu communication is critical for success in teaching. Managing small talk before classes and in office hours, handling students' questions, and fostering participation in recitations are just three of many contexts where TAs must be flexible and spontaneous in their interactions with students. The three-stage approach presented here helps TAs develop the verbal and nonverbal skills needed to interact confidently and appropriately in spontaneous interactions.

Novice TAs are intimidated at first but are overwhelmingly positive about the process after they have participated and have experienced and observed the impressive outcomes. In addition to increased confidence and flexibility, they develop a heightened awareness of the many layers of communication (including critical listening skills), as well as knowledge about their strengths and weaknesses as communicators. This three-stage approach is suitable as a regular activity in a semester-long program for TA development. For more limited contexts, with time constraints, Stage 1 alone or a combination of Stages 1 and 2 will work well.

Stage	1	2	3
Goals for students	• Develop awareness of process • Learn about constructive feedback • Build comfort level	• Focus message • Structure message • Use gambits • Fine-tune language	• Formalize tone • Increase interactions • Increase gambits • Manage feedback
Topics*	General	Discipline-related	Controversial
Focus of feedback	• Body language • Delivery (volume and pace)	• Organization • Direct approach • Gambits	• Treatment of feedback • Adjustment of tone

* A comprehensive list of topics is provided at the end of this activity.

Introductory Procedure for Instructor/Facilitator

1. Build motivation. Elicit from the TAs some contexts where effective impromptu speaking is required (e.g., interviews, discussion classes, teamwork, networking, socializing, teaching, lab supervision, office hours, mentoring, conference Q&A sessions).

2. Supply and flesh out the basic guidelines for impromptu speaking:
   • Anticipate context-specific topics, questions, and problems.
   • Speak briefly and directly.
   • Use appropriate gambits to buy time and organize comments.
   • Remember the power of nonverbal communication.

3. Define *constructive feedback*. In this context, constructive feedback is specific information about a speaker's strengths and weaknesses, including, if possible, suggestions for adjustments. Until students become accustomed to providing and receiving feedback, it is useful to coach them to use the following formula:

   Strength (e.g.) + Weakness (e.g.) = Constructive Feedback

For example, a constructive response to a Stage 1 impromptu might be: "You looked pretty confident to me. Your posture and gestures were natural. But you would have seemed even more confident if you had looked at people on both sides of the room. I felt a little left out."

Involving group members in providing brief reactions to the impromptus helps them develop critical listening skills and self-awareness. By extension, TAs develop more sensitive feedback mechanisms to use in their teaching. In the feedback sessions, I refrain from commenting unless I feel it is necessary to intervene, for two reasons: to encourage students to take their own reactions and analyses seriously, and to prevent them from depending excessively on my input. Instead, I provide a few written comments to each speaker as he or she sits down.

Procedure for TAs

1. After the question or topic is read aloud, a volunteer speaker goes to the front of the group, or a group member is "cold-called." Topics can be general—for example, "Describe the role of sports in your life" in Stage 1; discipline-specific: "Provide a brief explanation of nanofabrication" in Stage 2; or controversial: "Is it necessary to use animals in scientific research?" in Stage 3.

2. The speaker addresses the topic within one to two minutes.

3. The speaker stays in front of the group during the short constructive feedback session. By Stage 3, the speaker is expected to manage by eliciting comments and responding gracefully to them in the short feedback session. Ideally, a feedback session will involve at least two peers and will last no longer than three minutes.

Ongoing Procedure for Instructor/Facilitator

1. In Stage 1 the instructor has three tasks in addition to timekeeping: provide the question or topic; note several strengths and weaknesses to provide in writing to the speaker after peer feedback; and facilitate the peer feedback session.

2. In Stage 2 the instructor continues to keep track of time and provide the question or topic. In addition, he or she now encourages more detailed feedback (as outlined in the previous table) and provides more detailed written feedback. The instructor also encourages the speaker to initiate the feedback session.

3. In Stage 3 the instructor simply provides the question and keeps time.

Some Suggested Impromptu Topics

- Provide a brief definition of a key term in your discipline.
- In your opinion, what is the safest practical form of electrical power production?
- If you could go back in time to witness one historical event, what event would you choose? Why?
- Given the clear and serious health risks, do you think the sale of cigarettes should be illegal?
- Are you, or would you be, a potential organ donor?
- Is it necessary to use animals in scientific research?
- What should the United States be doing to deal with global warming?
- Can online education work?
- Describe the causes and results of the biggest failure in your life.
- Describe a typical weekday in your current life.
- How do you prepare to make important decisions?
- What are your main extracurricular interests?
- What are your major strengths and weaknesses?
- Canada is considering prohibiting cell phone use in public. Do you think this is a good policy? Why?
- Many companies have a dress code. Do you think employers should determine what kind of clothes employees should wear?
- A colleague of yours has asked you to provide the essentials of effective small talk for the work world. What pointers will you provide?
- Describe a time when group dynamics had a particularly good or bad effect on a team project in which you were involved.
- What would you tell a high school student who was considering applying to this university?
- What role should the United States play in the world?
- Describe a job interview that you've had.
- What are the major benefits of using email?
- What are the major dangers of using email?

- Provide the essential guidelines for using voice message machines. (Consider both the machine owner's and the caller's perspectives.)

- You are on the Admissions Committee for the class of 20_. Describe what you will look for in an admissions essay.

- Tell us about a book you have recently read. Why did you read it, what made it enjoyable or uninteresting? Would you recommend it?

- Describe your idea of the "perfect TA."

- Describe how the "perfect student" would behave in your tutorial.

- Participant use of laptops can help in classes and meetings, or it can create a distraction. How can we take advantage of the benefits and control the abuses of laptops in the classroom and workplace?

- Define *multitasking*. What helps you manage your work tasks efficiently?

- One task that job candidates are sometimes asked to do in an interview is to write an essay. Why do you think an employer would require an essay?

- As a job candidate, how would you respond if you were asked to write an essay on "What have you done this year that makes you proud?"

- Define *body language*. How can it contribute or detract from communication?

- Should companies be allowed to monitor their employees' email messages and web use?

- Describe a time when group dynamics had a particularly good or bad effect on a team project in which you were involved.

A TA Orientation Plenary Session on University Policies and Resources for Teaching

Derek Bruff

Vanderbilt University

GOALS

- To inform new TAs that there are likely to be difficult situations they will encounter as TAs, that these situations can be surprisingly complex, and that it is important to seek appropriate assistance when these situations occur
- To familiarize new TAs with a few university policies and resources related to teaching and to show them how to find out about other such policies and resources when they are needed

PREPARATION TIME

Approximately 6 hours to conduct interviews with campus experts, excerpt audio clips from those interviews, and construct the multimedia presentation to be used during the plenary session

EXECUTION TIME

60–90 minutes, depending on the number of scenarios used during the plenary session

RESOURCES

Information, brochures, or materials from various campus resource offices to supplement the multimedia presentation

Introduction

One goal of many new TA orientations is to familiarize new TAs with certain national and university policies related to teaching, such as the Family Educational Rights and Privacy Act (FERPA), institutional honor codes, and sexual harassment policies. A related goal is to familiarize new TAs with local resources that can assist them with difficult teaching situations, such as institutional equal opportunity, affirmative action, and disability services offices. Meeting these goals in interactive, engaging ways can be challenging, in part because new TAs often do not appreciate how important these policies and resources can be in the course of their future teaching duties.

In the orientation plenary session for new TAs described here, TAs reflect on possible responses to several difficult teaching scenarios (short, fictional case studies) related to some of these policies and resources. A key feature of this session is the use of audio clips of interviews with local campus experts discussing appropriate responses to the scenarios. Engaging TAs with these audio clips as well as with small and large group discussion about the scenarios can help them appreciate the complexity of these kinds of situations and the need to seek help when appropriate.

Procedure

Before the Plenary

1. Prior to the orientation session, identify a few key policies or resources that new TAs at your institution should know. Then write or locate a short scenario related to each policy or resource that could be encountered by new TAs at your institution. Each scenario should be brief and applicable to the TAs in your audience (which may include TAs from different disciplines and with different teaching duties). Each scenario should also include several possible responses to the scenario that TAs might make. Scenarios work best when more than one of the listed responses is reasonable and defensible. The following is an example of a scenario related to FERPA, a U.S. federal law designed to protect the privacy of student education records:

   > During your regular office hours in mid-October, the father of one of your first-year students calls. He explains that his daughter received a deficiency report in your course. The father is concerned about his daughter's adjustment to college, and he wants to talk with you about her performance in your class, asking specifically about attendance and grades. What should you say?
   >
   > - "I'll have to check with your daughter to make sure it's okay for me to discuss her grades with you."
   > - "I'm not at liberty to share that information. I encourage you to discuss this with your daughter."
   > - "Your daughter is an adult now and her grades are really none of your business. Goodbye."
   > - "Unfortunately, your daughter is doing poorly. She got a D on the first test and an F on the second."

2. For each scenario, interview a local faculty member or administrator familiar with the associated policy or resource, asking them to offer advice to new TAs in responding to the scenario. For the previous example, you might interview a staff member at your institution's

registrar's office familiar with FERPA and its enforcement on your campus. Audiotape the interview and, following the interview, select a brief excerpt from the interview, perhaps two or three minutes in length, to share during the plenary session.

3. Finally, prepare a multimedia presentation for use during the plenary that includes all of your scenarios, the audio clips from the expert interviews, and perhaps links to relevant campus web sites. Also prepare handouts with all of the scenarios to distribute to the new TAs at the plenary for note-taking purposes.

During the Plenary

1. During the session, spend about 20 minutes investigating each scenario with the new TAs in the following manner:

   • Present and read the scenario and possible responses to the new TAs.

2. Have each new TA discuss the scenario and his or her response to it with another TA in the session.

3. After a minute or two of this discussion in pairs, have the new TAs vote on their preferred response via a show of hands.

4. Then ask for a few volunteers to share with the large group their reasons for the response they chose. Echo and clarify their reasons to the group, but avoid evaluating their reasons at this time. Much of the complexity of the scenario is likely to become evident to the new TAs at this point.

5. Play the audio clip of the campus expert reflecting on the scenario. A short clip is likely to engage the new TAs, and including expert audio clips can be more efficient than bringing in guest speakers during the session.

6. Briefly review the expert's response to the scenario and mention any relevant points the expert made during the interview that were not included in the audio clip.

7. Point the new TAs to local resources that might provide help in similar situations. Assembling a list of such resources (for all scenarios as well as other situations not included in the scenarios) in a handout or web site can be useful.

8. Take questions from the audience as time permits.

9. Repeat this process with each of the scenarios.

Variations

A variety of scenarios and experts can be used in this kind of session, depending on the policies and resources most important to new TAs at your institution. Including multiple scenarios focusing on the same policy or resource is also an option, as the TAs' responses to later scenarios will tell you what they learned during the discussion of earlier cases. One might also include a scenario that calls for TAs to determine which of several policies or resources is most relevant.

If each scenario has more than one reasonable and defensible response, then asking new TAs to vote via a show of hands is sufficient. However, use of a classroom response system (sometimes called "clickers") or similar technology can facilitate anonymous responses from the TAs, preventing the bias that results when an audience member sees how other audience members are voting before casting his or her own vote as well as making the environment safer for TAs to express dissenting opinions. Such systems often make it possible to display a histogram of responses to the new TAs that can add to the engagement TAs have with the activity.

Teaching in Computer Classrooms

Shaun K. Kane, Joe Hannah,
Phillip M. Edwards, Jennie Dorman
University of Washington

GOALS

By the end of this workshop, participants should be able to:

- Identify goals and challenges of computer classroom instruction.
- Identify and discuss effective strategies for teaching in computer classrooms.
- Identify key objectives for the first week of class and begin to create a plan for that week.

PREPARATION TIME

1 to 2 hours to assemble any necessary resources

EXECUTION TIME

75 minutes

RESOURCES

- Index cards containing potential topics for practice lab sessions
- Worksheet with a list of objectives for the activity

Introduction

The audience for the workshop described here ranges in size from 20–35 participants, over half of whom have had less than one year of formal teaching experience. The Teaching in Computer Classrooms workshop introduces TAs to some of the challenges posed by computer classroom environments and provides an opportunity to discuss strategies that can be used to address these challenges. This workshop may be held in a traditional classroom or in a computer lab. A traditional classroom is a comfortable environment for large and small group discussion and allows participants to focus on teaching strategies without being distracted by lab equipment. However, conducting the workshop in a computer classroom may highlight some of the challenges inherent in conducting discussions and group activities in such an environment. Because computing resources and classroom environments may differ between departments, the lab format might work best for workshops held within a single department.

Procedure

Stage 1 (15–25 minutes)

1. Begin the workshop by highlighting the diversity of pedagogical techniques that can be used in computer classrooms. Ask participants to share their prior experiences as teachers or students within their disciplines. As TAs discuss their experiences, point out similarities or differences in the experiences and perspectives they describe.

   Variation for step 1. Instead of having participants reflect on prior experiences, ask them to describe the course(s) they anticipate teaching in the future.

2. Identify general goals of computer classroom instruction and common concerns instructors have about computer classrooms. Ask each participant to share one question or concern about computer classroom teaching or to generate a list of concerns in small groups.

3. As the participants describe their concerns, note common issues on the board or an overhead transparency in order to track the discussion; some common concerns might include 1) managing the instructor's visibility to students in an environment with many distractions, 2) monitoring student progress and keeping students on-task, 3) resolving unexpected difficulties with hardware and software, and 4) supporting students with varying levels of experience with computer technologies. Since TAs are likely to have questions related to lab technology or policy, you may want to prepare a handout with common technical information for the campus—for example, general contact information for classroom technical support—recognizing that departmental support for computing technologies may vary.

4. At the end of the activity, ask participants to spend five minutes brainstorming solutions in small groups to some of the concerns that were raised.

   Variation for step 4. Another option is to extract solutions from a handout or overhead on which you present feedback from students about what helps them learn in computer classrooms (e.g., a selection of quotes like "I like how there is an explanation of the assignment in the beginning of class, and then he walks around and answers questions"). Featuring student voices can be helpful, both by providing concrete strategies for improving teaching and by emphasizing the impact that these strategies can have on student learning.

Stage 2 (30–40 minutes)

1. Ask participants to form small groups and plan a short computer classroom activity. Encourage groups to choose an activity topic that interests them, but provide some generic activity ideas (on index cards) for groups that need help choosing a topic. These can include introductory computer lab activities such as downloading a file from the classroom web page, activating a university email account, or emailing a Microsoft Word document to the instructor. Providing time in the workshop for new TAs to consider how they will teach these basic skills helps them address their students' uneven preparation for working with technology, one of the challenges discussed earlier in the workshop.

   Variation for step 1. Because some participants may prefer to plan an activity that is more specific to their future teaching roles, you might group participants with other TAs from their department. If it is not feasible to group TAs by department, you might group TAs from departments that use similar software or teaching styles. For example, TAs from math, engineering, and computer science may all use scientific computing software such as MATLAB, and many departments use web authoring software such as Adobe Dreamweaver or Photoshop. You might also provide groups with contextual information about the activity they are planning, such as hypothetical class sizes, classroom configurations, or ranges of student experience levels with the relevant technologies.

2. Give groups 10–15 minutes to work on their lesson plans, encouraging them to address the concerns, goals, and strategies discussed earlier in the workshop. Each group should sketch out a plan for the classroom period by allocating time for introduction, lecture materials, lab exercises, and other parts of the classroom activity. A structured activity worksheet can help draw attention to some of the important issues. For example, you might provide groups with a worksheet with the following questions:
   - What is the topic of the lab activity?
   - What are the important take-home points for this topic?
   - What is the expected technical and domain experience of the students? How will you address students with more or less experience?
   - How will you set up the classroom space and manage student groups?

- What kinds of instructional materials (handouts, slides, etc.) will you provide?
- How will you handle the concerns we discussed previously?

3. When the groups are ready, give each group the opportunity to present their proposed lesson plan or to share any new questions, concerns, and insights that arose in the activity. Provide time for the other groups to respond with questions and suggestions. In the context of a post-discussion debriefing, ask group members specific questions about how their lesson plans address the concerns discussed earlier in the workshop—for example, you might ask, "How would you respond if a group of students started surfing the web?" or "Do you have a plan to accommodate students who have trouble with basic computer use?"

Stage 3 (15–20 minutes)

1. The goal of the final part of the workshop is to assist TAs in generating plans and to-do lists to prepare for the first week of class. Ask participants to consider the development of their classroom policies (e.g., when the TA will be available by email, what students can expect from the TA, what the TA expects of students, how students can obtain help related to the relevant technologies, etc.). To aid participants in doing this, present examples of classroom policies or first-day lesson plans written by experienced TAs.

   Variation for step 1. Alternatively, ask participants to generate a list of tasks they need to complete before they begin the term. You might provide a partial list of activities (e.g., visiting the classroom ahead of time to collect information about the physical space and the setup of the lab environment, talking to TAs who have taught previous versions of the course, setting up user accounts for their students, etc.) and ask participants to adapt the list for their own use. Allow participants to work alone or in groups, and provide a worksheet with the following sections for them to complete: 1) tasks to complete before the first day, 2) items to bring on the first day, and 3) how to set the tone for the first day.

2. In the final five minutes of the workshop, stress that TAs have many strategies available to them when teaching in computer classrooms, briefly review some of the main points raised during the discussions, and encourage participants to make use of the generated artifacts in their future teaching roles.

Teaching in Lab Settings

**Jennie Dorman, Michelle Smith,
Sara O'Brien, Karen Freisem**
University of Washington

GOALS

By the end of this workshop, participants should be able to:
- Determine goals and identify challenges of lab instruction.
- Recognize and practice using effective strategies for teaching in labs.
- Identify key components of a successful first day of class.

PREPARATION TIME

A minimum of 2 hours to assemble any necessary resources

EXECUTION TIME

75 minutes

RESOURCES

For the practice pre-lab activity, you will need several sets of complex instructions such as recipes or automotive repair instructions, one for every four to six participants, plus a couple of blank transparencies and overhead pens for each group (see notes in procedure section). You will also need prepared transparencies listing any questions you want the group to discuss. Finally, we recommend distributing a handout on which you summarize key points, make additional suggestions, and pose questions to help participants plan their first day of class.

Introduction

The audience for this workshop is science and engineering TAs, most of whom have had less than one year of formal teaching experience and who will be teaching in laboratory settings.

Procedure

Stage 1 (10–20 minutes)

1. To engage TAs in the workshop, give participants three minutes to write an answer to or talk to their neighbor about one or two of the following questions:
   - What questions/concerns do you have about teaching in labs?
   - What do you remember about the lab classes you took?

- What are some of the factors that make it challenging to learn (or teach) in lab settings?
- What could your previous lab instructors have done differently to make the learning experience better for you?

As volunteers share their responses, compile a list on the board or overhead, using these concerns/reflections as entry points for a discussion of strategies that are effective in lab settings.

Variation for step 1. If you have access to written feedback from students at your institution about what helps them learn in lab settings, displaying a few representative quotes may provide a helpful way to begin the workshop by focusing on student learning outcomes. For example, we have used a list of student responses to the question "What has helped you learn in this lab section?" (including such responses as "The way you help us out by prodding us along without telling us the answer," "You know what you are talking about and you are willing to work with us until we understand it completely," and "Your extra questions were very helpful and made us stop and think about why we were doing each step—which is really the whole point.") Ask workshop participants to read each quote aloud, then ask the group to extract from these quotes the strategies each TA employed. Use their replies to start a list of strategies or issues to discuss later in the session.

2. Ask participants to jot down what they see as the goals of lab instruction.

3. Debrief as a full group, listing lab instruction goals on the board and adding any others you think are important. Commonly cited goals include providing students hands-on experience with experimental processes, developing students' understanding of course concepts, and developing students' teamwork skills.

4. Set up the rest of the workshop by posing the question "What can we do as instructors to help achieve these goals?"

Stage 2 (40–50 minutes)

1. Because presenting a short introduction to lab exercises is a key responsibility of TAs in many laboratory classes, give participants the chance to practice designing and delivering a pre-lab talk. Participants often cite this hands-on practice as the most valuable

experience they have in the workshop. To begin, provide a handout with some suggestions about how to introduce labs clearly and efficiently. We include suggestions such as the following: state the goal of the lab, tie the lab exercise in with lecture material or previous labs, incorporate props or visual aids, and highlight any special instructions or safety considerations.

2. Divide participants into groups of four to six, either by discipline or in mixed groups. In general, we prefer mixed groups because students from different disciplines tend to focus on different parts of the activity.

3. Give each group a unique set of instructions about which they must prepare a short pre-lab presentation. Selecting the topics for these presentations is tricky because the TAs attending this workshop come from a wide variety of scientific and engineering disciplines. We use topics like elaborate recipes or automotive repair instructions, which—while broadly accessible—allow participants to practice introducing complex procedures. To help new TAs make the connection between this activity and their own teaching contexts, choose instructions/recipes that resemble common lab procedures. For example, you can provide instructions on how to devein a shrimp (noting the resemblance to a dissection), make mayonnaise (likening it to a titration), make sauerkraut (a microbiology lab), or change a car's spark plugs (akin to an engineering lab).

4. Tell participants they'll have 10–12 minutes to plan their pre-lab presentation. Provide each group with a blank overhead and pens, and tell them that each group member must speak during the presentation so everyone can benefit from the public-speaking practice.

5. Have each group present their three-minute pre-lab presentation. After each presentation, briefly comment on the things the groups did well. To finish the workshop on time, you will need to keep your feedback very brief (not more than one minute per group). One efficient way to provide feedback is to refer back to the list of suggestions that you provided at the start, noting the strategies on this list that the group used effectively in their presentation.

Variation for step 5. If you have a little more time, ask the other participants what elements they thought were particularly effective and assemble a list of suggestions from their comments (rather than providing it at the outset).

6. Now that participants have practiced delivering a pre-lab talk, help them plan their first day of class. Talk briefly about the topics that lab instructors often discuss on the first day, and show an example first-day lesson plan or lab section syllabus.

7. Distribute a handout with planning questions for the first day of the course for participants to answer. We have used the following questions, chosen for their relevance to a range of disciplines and their utility even to graduate students who don't know yet what they'll be teaching:

   • How will you introduce yourself on the first day of class? Write down three or four things you'll mention about yourself—for example, your name (how you want students to address you), status ("I'm a graduate student in . . ."), any experiences that relate to the course (teaching, jobs, research, hobbies), what you like about the subject of the class (because students report that instructor enthusiasm is an important motivator), and so on.

   • What information do you want to collect about your students (e.g., how do they want to be addressed, previous experience with this topic or prerequisites taken, why they're taking this class, hobbies)? And how will you collect it (e.g., on index cards, orally, via email, via online survey tool)?

   • Articulating your expectations: What do you expect of your students? What are your ground rules for class? What can your students expect of you (e.g., the best way to reach you, when you will and won't check email, how you see your role in the lab)?

8. Give participants a few minutes to write their own answers to some or all of the questions, and then debrief as a group or in pairs.

Stage 3 (10–15 minutes)

1. Lab course work typically involves students working in groups, and one of the big challenges of serving as a TA for a lab class is managing these group dynamics. To explore this subject, present several scenarios such as the following:

   • One group in your lab section will not stop asking you questions. How do you get them to work more independently without seeming unhelpful?

- You notice a student who is not participating with his or her group. How can you get that student involved?
- A frustrated student is asking you a question but you don't understand what the student is asking. How should you respond to the student in a way that minimizes his or her frustration but allows you to keep the lab progressing?

2. Have the whole class brainstorm strategies for dealing with these scenarios while you or a volunteer records the resulting strategies.

   Variation for step 2. Alternatively, you could divide students into small groups and ask each group to brainstorm responses to one of the scenarios, then regroup and debrief as a whole class, adding in your own ideas and tips.

3. Distribute a handout summarizing key points about teaching in labs. The handout we use highlights specific strategies for encouraging students to work well in groups, for monitoring and guiding student progress, for the first day of class, and for introducing and wrapping up the lab.

4. Discuss the handout briefly, highlighting certain strategies on it (especially those that address concerns expressed earlier in the workshop), adding your own stories, and perhaps asking participants to volunteer anything else they've seen to be effective.

CHAPTER **TWO**

Advanced Skills

As teaching assistants (TAs) gain experience and confidence in their classroom skills, they are ready to begin thinking beyond the day-to-day necessities of teaching. Activities that may have seemed too daunting at first, such as group work and active learning, are now within their reach. They can begin to understand the importance of certain pedagogical decisions like setting course goals and determining the appropriate pace, and they can use their experience to participate in such decision-making. The key to helping TAs excel is to remember that becoming an effective teacher is a developmental process, but it does not happen on its own. Carefully planned support and challenges are critical to the acquisition of new skills at all stages of a teaching career. The activities presented in this chapter are examples of the kinds of skills that can be developed once the basics are mastered.

Classroom Management Skills: Expanding Your Repertoire

Lee Warren
Harvard University

GOALS
To extend one's techniques for handling classroom situations

PREPARATION TIME
None

EXECUTION TIME
2 hours or less

RESOURCES
Recording and playback equipment

Introduction

All teaching can be thought of as a string of choice points; at any moment you could stop the camera and think of five possibilities for how to proceed. Instructors are making choices all the time, whether consciously or unconsciously. This activity fosters awareness of choice points and leads to an expansion and enrichment of one's classroom management repertoire.

A teacher's success depends on the following key features: 1) the knowledge that there is not one right way to teach nor one right template to apply in all classroom situations, and 2) the flexibility to use a range of techniques to meet situations as they arise, so responses can be adapted to individual students in the particular context of any given class. Applying the same technique to every student, without regard for her particular strengths, weaknesses, and needs, can do more damage than good. The technique described here helps instructors develop a range of possible responses. When used in videotape viewings, this strategy is one way to help TAs recognize and practice these key features of effective teaching.

Procedure

1. One of the TA's classes is recorded via a video or DVD camera.

2. The TA meets individually to view the recording with a consultant or instructor.

3. The instructor stops the recording at specific points where the TA has handled a challenging moment, e.g., an unresponsive or monopolizing student, a wrong answer, a serious digression, or a question that the TA is unable to answer.

4. The instructor identifies the technique that the TA has used in each challenging moment, and elicits as many alternative responses as possible. We usually aim for five possible responses.

Variations

This procedure could also be used in a group session with a preselected recorded clip.

Determining Appropriate Course Goals and Pacing: An Exercise for Advanced TAs

Allyson Polsky McCabe, Lu Zhang

Johns Hopkins University

GOALS

To encourage beginning instructors to:

- Identify courses that are appropriate for mixed-level undergraduate learners.
- Conceptualize courses as delivery mechanisms for integrated analytical skills acquisition, not merely disciplinary content mastery.

PREPARATION TIME

Before the workshop, TAs must select a syllabus (their own or another's) to bring to the workshop for instructor and peer critique.

EXECUTION TIME

1.5 hours

RESOURCES

Access to a range of past and current syllabi from a core or otherwise frequently offered departmental course

Introduction

There are numerous templates available to assist beginning instructors with the mechanics of syllabus design (e.g., contact information, text requirements, grading procedures, class policies, and schedules). However, beyond filling in the basic matrix and determining what topics and texts to cover, instructors also need to consider the prior knowledge base and instructional needs of various learners (nonmajors, majors, and majors who may be prospective graduate students). Unfortunately, beginning instructors—who are often current graduate students or recent Ph.D.s—tend to teach their courses at their own learning level, although the majority of their students are unprepared to perform at that depth or pace. The purpose of this activity is to introduce beginning instructors to the concept of skills-based learning and to provide them with experiential instruction in identifying exemplary syllabi. A secondary purpose is to lay the groundwork for further instruction in syllabus and assignment design. This activity works best when conducted in a small group of students from the same discipline. Ideally, it should be conducted the semester before TAs are expected to independently teach their first course.

Procedure

1. The workshop instructor provides the group with detailed guidelines that are used to critique course syllabi.

2. Working in teams of two or three, participants discuss a syllabus with particular attention paid to identifying skills that students are implicitly expected to 1) have prior to the course, 2) acquire through in-class instruction, or 3) gain independently during the semester.

3. The next stage involves determining the extent to which course texts, class meetings, assignments, and examinations appear to help build, reinforce, and test these skills. Special attention is paid to organization and pacing.

4. The teams present their findings to the group and alternative structuring is suggested as necessary throughout the guided discussion.

Developing Effective Consulting Skills

Michele Marincovich, Marcelo Clerici-Arias,

Mariatte Denman, Robyn Wright Dunbar

Stanford University

GOALS

To develop teaching consultation skills for graduate teaching consultants and to mentor TAs

PREPARATION TIME

Little or none beyond preparation of handouts

EXECUTION TIME

Approximately 60 minutes (as the opening segment of a half-day consultant training session)

ASSUMPTIONS

That graduate students new in this role will have *exceptional teaching abilities,* but may not have thought deeply or practically about how these abilities translate into the attributes needed to be an *exceptional teaching consultant*

RESOURCES

The following handouts:
- "Effective Teachers." This sample handout is included here, but we recommend customizing it to your own institution. The categories and items were chosen to match those of our end-of-term student evaluations so that consultants and mentor TAs are thinking about effective teaching within the same framework by which instructors are evaluated.
- "Characteristics of Effective Listening" by S. R. Phillips (in Bergquist & Phillips, 1977). This handout contrasts effective and ineffective listening behaviors.
- "Consultant Role-Playing Scenarios." This handout, which is included here, contains brief guidelines and some sample cases that consultants might experience. The sample scenarios may be customized to your own institution.

Introduction

Stanford University's Center for Teaching and Learning offers a consultant program for graduate students interested in enriching their teaching experience and contributing to departmental and university-wide teaching dialogues. Consultants are highly experienced, often award-winning TAs selected on the basis of outstanding teaching evaluations and interpersonal skills. After training, these graduate students provide peers with one-on-one teaching consultations, mid-quarter student evaluations, and class-room/videotaped observation and analysis. They may also co-develop and offer university-wide or departmental practice teaching sessions and teaching workshops.

The goal of the effective consulting activity is to kick off a discussion about the skills needed in a consulting situation by first guiding new consultants to make explicit their own ideas about effective teaching and then helping them transfer these understandings to an effective consulting role (e.g., developing listening, diagnostic, and problem-solving abilities; considering different roles such as peer advisor, mentor, and coach).

Procedure

1. Thinking individually, participants list attributes of effective teaching. (2 minutes)

2. If the group is large (e.g., larger than 12), share thoughts with a neighbor and create a list of three high-priority attributes. If the group is small, move on to the next step. (3 minutes)

3. Discussion with the full group: Create a brainstorming list and then place the attributes into conceptual categories that participants help define. (10–15 minutes)

4. Introduce the notion that the attributes of effective teaching have been long studied and that an extensive literature exists in this area. Distribute the effective teaching handout with conceptual groupings based on end-of-term evaluations (e.g., organization and clarity, instructor-student interaction, etc.). Reemphasize that participants have a lot of background and good ideas about what constitutes effective teaching. Now, how prepared are they to transfer these understandings to their new *consulting* role? (10 minutes)

5. Looking at the worksheet summary and handout, which teaching attributes are also likely to be useful to a teaching consultant? Are there other attributes, perhaps not on the lists, that might be beneficial to a consultant? (Answers vary depending on what has been generated in the earlier steps, but should include listening/questioning skills, knowledge/experience, problem recognition, giving sensitive feedback, helping the instructor become a reflective problem solver, etc.) (10 minutes)

6. Questioning/listening role-play: Guided by the handouts "Characteristics of Effective Listening" and "Consultant Role-Playing Scenarios," consultant pairs take turns being TA and teaching consultant to role-play an initial consultation conversation about a teaching challenge the TA is facing. Pairs may use a common TA problem that we give them or one that they identify to discuss on their own. (20 minutes)

7. Debrief this activity as a group. What was tough to do? What did a partner do well? What questions do you have about becoming an effective consultant? (10 minutes)

This discussion launches a half-day of more specific consultation exercises, including practice interpreting TA teaching video clips, leading student small group evaluations, and facilitating practice (or micro-) teaching sessions.

Variations

While we do this exercise with our center's new graduate teaching consultants, it would be equally useful in a workshop for departmental mentor TAs. When participant numbers merit, we have also added an observer role to the role-playing teams.

References

Phillips, S. R. (1977). Characteristics of effective listening. In W. H. Bergquist & S. R. Phillips (Eds.), *A handbook for faculty development* (Vol. 2, p. 207). Washington, DC: Council for the Advancement of Small Colleges.

EFFECTIVE TEACHERS

The following characteristics appear again and again in studies on, or discussions of, effective teachers. We have classified these qualities according to the broad categories and items that Stanford uses in course evaluations, which were in part based upon the work of M. Hildebrande, R.C. Wilson, and E.R. Dienst, *Evaluating University Teaching,* Berkeley: University of California, Center for Research and Development in Higher Education, 1971. Ken Bain's *What the Best College Teachers Do,* Cambridge: Harvard University Press, 2004, provides a nice update to this classic work.

Instructor's Organization and Clarity
- Sets out and meets clear objectives for the course and each class session
- Conveys thorough command of the field; knowledgeable about course material
- Explains clearly; uses examples, details, analogies, metaphors, and variety in modes of explanation
- Distinguishes between more important and less important points
- Presents material at an appropriate pace; knows whether or not the class is following the material and adjusts as needed

---

Instructor's Ability to Engage and Challenge Students
- Emphasizes conceptual understanding and/or critical thinking; poses intriguing and significant questions; assists students to think as scholars do
- Gives students a sense of the field, its past, present, and future directions, the origins of concepts and ideas
- Relates course topics to one another, to other courses, to other disciplines or fields; helps students connect course material to their own lives
- Discusses viewpoints other than his/her own; encourages independent thought and accepts criticism; challenges students to have and defend their own ideas

---

Instructor's Interaction with Students
- Demonstrates concern for student learning; enjoys teaching and is concerned about the quality of teaching
- Expects students to actively listen, think, and participate; stimulates, directs, and paces interactions with the class
- Is seen by students as approachable, available for consultation outside of class
- Seems genuinely interested in students; respects students as individuals
- Conveys a love of the field; is enthusiastic, inspiring, and motivating
- Is perceived as fair

Course Organization, Content, and Evaluation
- Selects course content that is valuable and worth learning
- Organizes course topics in a coherent fashion
- Creates diverse learning formats
- Chooses assignments that solidify understanding; sets and conveys clear and fair expectation for success

Consultant Role-Playing Scenarios

Scenario 1

A TA has come to you for a consultation about a recent unsuccessful teaching experience. Your role is to 1) listen carefully to the TA's story, 2) ask him or her several thoughtful questions, and 3) suggest, or brainstorm together, some solutions or alternative strategies.

Sample Experiences

- Students are not participating and the TA does all the talking.
- A few students are dominating and disrupting the section, contradicting the TA, and so on.
- Students are angry about bad grades on a recent exam and blame the TA.
- Students are unprepared and unmotivated.
- Choose another scenario you have seen or experienced.

Scenario 2

You are conducting a mid-quarter student small group evaluation (SGE) for a TA. Brainstorm responses to one or two of the following situations you may encounter.

When you visit the classroom:

- The TA is not ending class in time to do the SGE.
- There is not enough time left to do the SGE properly.
- Students give positive feedback and are reluctant to criticize their TA.
- Students give strong negative feedback, but in an emotionally charged or less-than-constructive manner.
- Other situations you can imagine or have experienced.

During your later consultation with the TA about the SGE results:

- The TA seems resistant or indifferent to student feedback (e.g., when the SGE and consultation are required rather than personally requested).

- The biggest problem students raise in the class is out of the TA's control.
- The TA is surprised by the feedback you give him or her.
- The SGE is given too late in the term to have much impact on the course.
- Other situations you can imagine or have experienced.

Interdisciplinary Soapbox

Jill Bible, Robyn Wright Dunbar
Stanford University

GOALS

To help TAs in interdisciplinary courses clarify and articulate the value of interdisciplinary thinking and practice an introductory "soapbox speech" explaining the role of an interdisciplinary TA

PREPARATION TIME

- 15 minutes to create participant worksheets
- 20 minutes to prepare facilitator introductory comments

EXECUTION TIME

60–90 minutes, depending on the number of participants

ASSUMPTIONS

TAs will understand the significance of setting early, clear expectations for a course and for student and TA roles, but may lack experience doing so for an interdisciplinary class in which these roles and expectations can differ from student experiences.

RESOURCES

Pens and worksheets

Introduction

TAs in interdisciplinary classes face some unique challenges. For example, TAs are expected to make connections across disciplines and help students to develop as integrative thinkers. Students, however, may expect TAs to provide "right" answers to "clear-cut" questions and demonstrate expert knowledge in all topic areas. While these may be appropriate expectations in disciplinary-based courses, they are challenging, if not counterproductive, to interdisciplinary learning goals.

Although many interdisciplinary TAs have reasons for their interest in interdisciplinary teaching and research, these reasons are often difficult to articulate. Taking the time to articulate the reasons for interdisciplinary thinking and the role of interdisciplinary TAs will help students understand the significance of, and gain appreciation for, interdisciplinarity. To practice this articulation, we develop "soapbox" pitches that TAs present on the first day of class. This activity can serve as the opening piece in a series of workshops to support interdisciplinary TAs in thinking critically about interdisciplinarity.

Procedure

1. The facilitator introduces the activity using reasoning such as that in the previous introductory paragraph. (5 minutes)

2. Hand out individual writing worksheets to participants. The top of the worksheet has the following paragraph:

   > Let's say you have three minutes to explain to your students why you think interdisciplinary learning is important and useful and how your role as a TA and their roles as students might be different in an interdisciplinary class. Use this as a figurative "soapbox" and justify your interdisciplinary pursuits!

   (Allow 10–15 minutes for response)

3. Write questions on the board (or worksheet) to help participants begin writing. For example:
   • How do you define interdisciplinarity? In your studies/work/course/field?
   • Why is interdisciplinary learning important?
   • What kinds of issues/topics/subject matter require it?
   • How do you justify an interdisciplinary approach to disciplinarians?
   • What do students typically expect of TAs? How does this compare to your role as an interdisciplinary TA?

4. Share soapbox pitches in small groups (three to four people). Each TA shares his or her pitch, gets feedback on clarity, missing parts, and so on. (20–30 minutes)

5. Individual redrafting. (10–20 minutes)

6. Share finished soapbox pitches with whole group. (15–20 minutes)

Variations

This activity can be altered slightly depending on the number of participants and the amount of time available.

1. To shorten the activity, you can ask only a few volunteers to share their soapbox pitches with the whole group.

2. To achieve more finished products, you can require TAs to arrive at the workshop with their first attempt at a soapbox pitch.

Introduction to Online Teaching and Learning: Using Asynchronous Discussions Effectively

Mary C. Wright
University of Michigan

GOALS
To introduce TAs to pedagogical strategies for effectively leading asynchronous online discussions

PREPARATION TIME
Minimal

EXECUTION TIME
25 minutes

RESOURCES
- A one-page excerpt of an online discussion (an example follows this activity)
- The facilitator may wish to distribute or refer participants to the following resources about online teaching and learning:
  - Tips for Teaching Online (www.itrc.wvu.edu/webct/faq20.html)
  - ADEC Guiding Principles for Distance Teaching and Learning (www.adec.edu/admin/papers/distance-teaching_principles.html)
  - Principles of Online Design (www.fgcu.edu/onlinedesign/Intro.html)

Introduction

Teaching and learning with technology is increasingly becoming a part of the postsecondary instructional climate. Asynchronous discussions are a good entry point to address teaching with technology for TAs as they illustrate general principles of best pedagogical practices, but they do not require as much skill to navigate as a fully online class, for example. This activity uses an authentic online discussion to allow participants to "discover" pedagogical strategies for teaching with technology.

Procedure

1. Participants read an excerpt of an online discussion (an example follows this activity).
2. In pairs, participants answer the following questions:
   - What is going well?
   - What is not going well?

- What role is the instructor playing?
- What could the instructor do differently?

3. A debrief collects participants' observations and strategies. If they are not raised in the discussion, points that could be highlighted by facilitators include:

- The instructor should ask questions at different levels (e.g., knowledge, comprehension, application, analysis, synthesis, and evaluation) so that the discussion develops.
- The instructor needs to provide clear instructions for students, including roles and responsibilities, goals of the discussion, appropriate and inappropriate behaviors, and standards for assessing student performance.
- To avoid the "clumping" that often happens with discussion boards right before the due date, the instructor could require two waves of discussion participation during a week, with staggered due dates.
- The instructor should be an active participant by clarifying, keeping the discussion on task, bringing in silent students and redirecting from students who may dominate, energizing the discussion, and bringing closure (i.e., summarizing).

Variations

If TAs are unfamiliar with discussion boards, the facilitator may wish to give more explanation of the technology and provide other examples. In addition, the clips found at http://pandora.cii.wwu.edu/showcase2000/smeins/showcase.htm may help to supplement the discussion as they depict one instructor who describes how she uses discussion boards.

Excerpt from an Online Discussion in a Social Work Class

Instructor (Wed., 11:06 a.m.): Erikson theorizes that young people face the psychosocial crisis of choosing intimacy or isolation. Briefly define both intimacy and isolation, and compare and contrast the experiences of those who successfully achieve intimacy and those who feel isolated.

Beth (Sat., 10:50 a.m.): In Erikson's theory, the crisis of intimacy versus isolation occurs in young adulthood (20s). During this period the person has achieved an individual identity, yet longs for the companionship and sharing of an intimate relationship. The ideal in this stage would be to have close relations with another that include the mutual exchange of ideas and values without judgment and a mutual respect for the other person with well-established boundaries and empathy between them.

On the other end of the scale, individuals who isolate themselves are cut off from this basic need. There is fear of intimacy, a blurring of boundaries, and a reluctance to become involved with another individual. "These people are afraid to share or express themselves in an intimate relationship" (text, p. 310). The text also states that isolation can be caused by one's circumstances in life, such as the intense desire for a particular career (e.g., doctor, lawyer, etc.), which would necessitate many years of intense study. Lastly, isolation can also occur within a marriage, as each partner moves in their own direction and suddenly finds themselves with nothing in common.

Instructor (Sun., 9:04 a.m.): Excellent answer, Beth.

Catherine (Sun., 4:11 p.m.): It's ironic that at the time when you want to share in a relationship with another, in today's world there is almost the same need for isolation because of the necessity for education and career. Perhaps it is the expectations within the relationship that cause the problems. For instance, that the relationship should be a full commitment versus a sharing of self and ideas without a full commitment, which would allow other pursuits. Traditional ideas of young relationships may be reaching a point where they don't fit with life goals. The possibility that they may not fit can cause self-doubt for the parties involved in the sharing. They must learn what and how much of themselves they can share and still fulfill their goals. There are many more lifestyles recognized as available today than there were 30 years ago.

Instructor (Mon., 7:28 a.m.): Catherine, good observation.

Yi (Mon., 9:56 a.m.): Beth, I agree with you, except in that last part. Isolation can occur in a marriage only if the relationship was based on intimacy. Intimacy deteriorates in a marriage only if the couple are not friends or married for all of the wrong reasons. You not only must love your spouse, but you must like them as well.

Ed (Sun., 11:58 a.m.): Yi, I couldn't agree more! Although I have been married for only 3 years, my wife and I are best friends. We have been since before we were "together." That is the most important part of a relationship in my opinion. If you base your relationship on "intimacy," when that "intimacy" fades, the relationship fades with it. If your relationship is as important as your physical intimacy, the entire relationship is complete. I not only love my wife, I really like her.

Claudia (Wed., 8:51 p.m.): I'm beginning to feel stuck in isolation right now; it seems that every waking moment, which has been sometimes 16 hours, is spent on a computer. Even though I have 2 midterms, 2 research papers, a journal, more web board work, dishes to wash, clothes to fold, and no job. I think I will call a loved one and get intimate. Thanks for the wake-up call. I'll let you know before I feel guilty and eat the box of ice cream sandwiches and the bag of Amos's Chocolate Chip-Pecan Cookies I just bought.

Thanks to Erping Zhu, Center for Research on Learning and Teaching, University of Michigan, for this transcript.

Reaction and Response: Group Problem Solving and Effective Feedback

Jane Dunphy

Massachusetts Institute of Technology

GOALS

- To introduce TAs to techniques that foster students' active engagement in their own learning
- To encourage awareness of small group dynamics
- To practice providing constructive feedback in group problem-solving activities

PREPARATION TIME

None

EXECUTION TIME

45–60 minutes

ASSUMPTIONS

TAs have been introduced to the basics of active learning, group dynamics, and constructive feedback.

Introduction

Research over the past 20 years has taught us that learning is an active process in which students engage continuously, constructing meaning as they go. We know that context has a great impact on learning, that problems motivate learning, and that both stimulation and reflection are necessary for substantive learning to take place. Techniques that foster active learning motivate students to engage, increase learning of course content and problem solving, develop teamwork and communication skills, and provide more feedback to instructors than traditional lecturing.

The activity described here allows TAs from across disciplines to experience group work while focusing on group dynamics. At the same time, it provides an opportunity for one or more TAs to facilitate a debriefing session with constructive feedback on the groups' solutions.

Procedure

Stage 1

1. Participants work individually for approximately 5–10 minutes to establish an approach to solving an approximation task, for example:

- Number of wine bottle corks in a 16-gallon barrel
- Number of soccer balls to cover the field (one layer) of a standard soccer stadium
- Number of baseballs to cover a standard baseball diamond (one layer)

(Billy Koen of the University of Texas at Austin and Karl Smith of the University of Minnesota have used similar activities in teaching first-year engineering students to model problems. A typical group task requires students to approximate the number of ping pong balls that would fit into their classroom.)

2. TAs then work in groups of three or four. One member of each group observes and makes notes on the group interactions while the others work to arrive at one answer (approximately 10 minutes).

3. The observer in each group leads a debriefing session about the group dynamics during the process.

Stage 2

1. One member of each group writes the group's problem-solving strategy on the board. Depending on the number of groups and the availability of board space, the representative group members can go to the board one at a time or at the same time. If the groups' strategies are placed on the board beside each other, the focus stays on the approximation task and is deflected from the individuals who provide the solutions.

2. Playing the role of a recitation TA, a volunteer participant reviews the solutions on the board and provides feedback. This activity allows the volunteer to practice interpreting and responding to the groups' different problem-solving processes and different solutions in a respectful, flexible, and academically rigorous manner. Depending on the number of groups, several participants could take turns acting as the recitation TA providing feedback.

Teaching Practice: Emphasis on Active Learning

Tershia Pinder

University of Michigan

GOALS

- To give TAs practice in getting students actively engaged and participating in lectures
- To allow TAs to reflect on their teaching by reviewing the video and answering reflection questions
- To provide TAs with immediate peer feedback on student understanding

PREPARATION TIME

A 20-minute introduction to the practice teaching format and active learning strategies

EXECUTION TIME

- Total time is approximately 90 minutes for a group of five TAs. To train large numbers of TAs simultaneously, several moderators would have to be recruited. For example, 120 TAs will need approximately 24 moderators.
- For each TA, it takes between 12–17 minutes for each presentation and feedback session (7-minute lesson with 5–10 minute feedback).

ASSUMPTIONS

- TAs have reviewed resources on ways to implement active learning strategies prior to the session.
- Moderators have been trained on ways to give constructive feedback and how to facilitate the practice teaching session.

RESOURCES

None

Introduction

The most common form of delivering information to students is through the traditional lecture. However, research shows that students' attention span wanes within approximately 15 minutes (Johnstone & Percival, 1976). Because lectures still predominate, it is useful for TAs to develop skills in the enhanced lecture, which is "a series of short mini-lectures punctuated by specific active learning events designed to meet class objectives" (Bonwell, 1996, p. 33). Empirical research has shown that active learning is an approach that can promote student engagement and clarify misconceptions when it is designed around learning objectives (Prince, 2004). Active learning techniques give students the opportunity to think critically about the material. They can determine what they know, show their understanding of the material, apply their knowledge, analyze relationships, and synthesize ideas to form a new whole. In addition, students can work together in groups to answer a question, solve a problem, and/or compare ideas.

To give TAs the opportunity to develop this skill, a practice teaching session can be used to simulate a mini-classroom experience. By videotaping the session, TAs can view themselves as others see them and reflect on the effectiveness of their presentation. With the help of the facilitator, TAs can reflect on and discuss the strengths and areas of improvement for the lesson. Further, the TA can receive feedback from peers as to the effectiveness of the active learning strategies used and their alignment with course goals. In sum, this session promotes student-centered teaching methods, self-assessment of one's teaching, and, through peer feedback, information on student learning and their own performance.

Procedure

Before Class

1. Select a topic. The TA decides on the topic for the lesson by asking, "What do I want to teach my students?" The choice of topic stems from an array of possibilities: his or her research area, the class he or she will teach, or a hobby. The main purpose is for the TA to feel comfortable delivering the information and implementing active learning without focusing solely on the topic.

2. Determine goals for the lesson. "What do I want students to know, to be able to do, and to feel by the end of the lesson?"

3. Develop a creative introduction. To stimulate interest and thinking, the TA is encouraged to prepare a handout or an overhead to help clarify the material. Important questions to reflect on include, "What are some real-world examples or practical applications for this subject?" and "What are some historical or personal anecdotes that would motivate student interest?"

4. Design questions to ask the class. The TA writes down precisely how to state the questions and is prepared to paraphrase them during the class session to have more than one way to ask the same question. In addition, the TA can predict the answers to the questions.

5. Plan an activity to actively engage students. The TA reviews information on active learning strategies for assistance and decides precisely what students should do and plans clear instructions for the task

6. Develop a conclusion. The TA plans how to conclude the lesson using students' work whenever possible. The TA can ask, "What are the main points I want to summarize?"

During Class

1. The moderator begins the session by reminding the participants that each TA is expected to deliver a seven-minute, interactive lesson with active learning. TAs may take a few minutes to review their lesson. Then the moderator demonstrates the video camera operation. Each TA will serve as a videographer for one of their peers. Next, the moderator determines an order of presentation by asking for volunteers and writes the list on the board. The first TA on the list should give his or her lesson, while the last TA on the list works the camera.

2. Each TA presents a seven-minute lesson that is videotaped. While the TA delivers the presentation, the audience members (a moderator and fellow TAs) take notes as needed and act as students. After the TA finishes, the next TA presents a lesson and the first TA operates the camera. Rotate in this way, with each TA first giving a lesson then working the camera for the next presentation, until everyone has finished giving their lessons. The moderator uses the timer and when the seven minutes have passed, thanks the TA and invites him or her to sit down. If the TA ends before the seven minutes are up, the moderator waits until the timer beeps to thank him or her. This gives the moderator an opportunity to stress that teachers need to carefully practice time management.

3. After all TAs in a room have presented their session, the TAs view the tapes to see themselves in action, to reflect on their teaching, and to receive feedback from their peers. During the playback, the audience will complete a feedback form to answer the following two questions: What went well? and What could you do differently next time? The moderator in the room will ask the TA and then the audience to respond to the first question and then to second question.

The feedback forms completed by the audience will be given to the TA at the conclusion of the exercise.

Variations

When it is not possible to give TAs adequate time to prepare an active learning activity, a five-minute mini-lesson on a topic of their choice could be used. With the reduction in teaching time, the lesson focuses on delivering an explanation instead of incorporating active learning.

Depending on the resources available, this session could be taped. The TA would have five minutes to explain the topic, and the moderator would use a timer to reinforce the need for proper time management. Once again, audience members would take notes as if they were students in the class. Unlike the taped practice teaching sessions, the peer feedback happens immediately after the lesson for a session that is not being recorded.

Acknowledgements

This program has been developed based upon the work of staff members from the Center for Research on Learning and Teaching since 2002.

References

Bonwell, C. C. (1996). Enhancing the lecture: Revitalizing a traditional format. In T. E. Sutherland & C. C. Bonwell (Eds.), *Using active learning in college classes: A range of options for faculty* (pp. 31–44). San Francisco, CA: Jossey-Bass.

Johnstone, A. H., & Percival, F. (1976, March). Attention breaks in lecture. *Education in Chemistry, 13*(2), 49–50.

Prince, M. (2004, July). Does active learning work? A review of the research. *Journal of Engineering Education, 93*(3), 223–231.

Taped Practice Teaching Session
Focus on Active Learning
Peer Feedback Form

Please describe the strengths of this lesson:

Please provide suggestions to this teacher:

Please rate the following items using the scale by marking the appropriate column.	Needs Improvement	Satisfactory	Well Done	Not Observed
Introduction: The lesson was introduced in an interesting and effective way, and the goal or purpose of the lesson was clear.				
Level: The lesson was presented at an appropriate level for the intended audience.				
Content: The content was developed in an organized manner, emphasizing important points. Examples or applications helped students relate material to familiar concepts.				
Introduction for active learning: Directions were clear and understandable. Students had an opportunity to report back or use outcomes in class discussion.				
Effectiveness of active learning: The instructor effectively involved the students actively in the lesson.				
Purpose of active learning: The learning activity had an appropriate place in the lesson and its purpose was clear.				
Climate: The instructor established a positive climate of approachability, setting an appropriate tone for the instructor-student relationship.				
Enthusiasm: The instructor showed enthusiasm for the subject and introduced interesting aspects of the content.				
Questions: The instructor checked for student understanding and invited student questions. When questions were asked, the instructor responded clearly and willingly.				
Visual aids: The instructor used the board and/or other visuals effectively.				
Time management: The pace of the lesson was appropriate and the instructor managed the time well and brought the lesson to a logical conclusion.				

CHAPTER **THREE**

Professional Development

As teaching assistants (TAs) prepare to move into academic careers beyond the classroom, they need assistance in learning how to document and talk about their teaching. These kinds of workshops prepare graduate students to move through the job application process, interviews, and conference presentations with certainty and professionalism. As new faculty members on their new campuses, they are ready to participate actively in self-evaluation and peer evaluation processes, and to be teaching resources for the departments in which they are housed.

ASPECTS: Advancing Students' Professional Excellence with Certificates in Teaching Series

Mark Decker

University of Texas at Austin

GOALS

To provide opportunities for students to conceptualize the incorporation of teaching best practices into their course design

PREPARATION TIME

For workshop instructors: no more than 10 minutes to set up the room for each of three core sessions

EXECUTION TIME

- For workshop instructors: Delivery of three associated core sessions of approximately 75 minutes each. In addition, the instructor spends approximately 30 minutes scoring submitted essays.
- For participants: Attendance at three associated core sessions of approximately 75 minutes each. In addition, participants are expected to attend two elective sessions of the same duration. Participants also spend the necessary time, up to several hours, writing the essay associated with each series for which they want certificate consideration.

RESOURCES

- For workshop instructors: Rubric
  (www.utexas.edu/academic/diia/gsi/aspects/scoring_rubric.pdf)
- For participants: Instructions and question
  (www.utexas.edu/academic/diia/gsi/aspects/essay_instr.pdf)
- Example of an essay that does not meet requirements
  (www.utexas.edu/academic/diia/gsi/aspects/essay_score3.pdf)
- Example of a passing essay
  (www.utexas.edu/academic/diia/gsi/aspects/essay_score5.pdf)

Introduction

ASPECTS encourages ongoing pedagogical, personal, and professional development throughout the career of Graduate Student Instructors (GSIs). During the fall and spring semesters, GSIs will have the opportunity to attend ASPECTS sessions presented by teaching, learning, assessment, and technology professionals. Each semester, sessions are offered at two different times and days of the week to best meet the students' scheduling needs.

Procedure

1. Students may choose to work toward a certificate in any or all of the following series:
   - Assessment: The assessment certificate will enable the GSI to appropriately use multiple assessment modes and approaches aligned with learning objectives to assess student learning before, during, and after instruction.
   - Leading Discussions: The leading discussions certificate will enable the GSI to design, implement, and evaluate effective discussion.
   - Lecturing: The lecturing certificate will enable the GSI to design lectures that are based on key communication skills and learning theory, to consider the needs of students, and to increase student understanding through the use of appropriate active learning techniques.
   - Teaching Research Skills: The teaching research skills certificate will enable the GSI to apply best practices to library research assignments; teach students how to find, evaluate, and synthesize information effectively and ethically; and structure courses to prevent plagiarism.
   - Teaching with Technology: The teaching with technology certificate will enable the GSI to design a course that incorporates technology to manage course materials, facilitate discussion, and promote active learning.
   - Understanding Your Students: The understanding your students certificate will enable the GSI to design instruction that takes into account student differences in order to promote individual motivation for learning, accommodate different learning styles, and broaden the use of more effective learning strategies.

   Example: If a student decides to strive toward an assessment certificate, he or she would have to attend the following three core sessions. These are listed with their descriptions and the expected session outcomes:
   - *Using rubrics to grade student performance.* When grading "subjective" assignments such as essays, projects, and portfolios, students

often complain that the grading standards are vague, inconsistent, or unfair. In this workshop we will explore ways to make the grading process more objective using a systematic scoring guideline called a "rubric." We will discuss rubrics and their essential components, various types of rubrics, how to select pre-made rubrics, and how to create a rubric. You will also have some hands-on activities to develop your own sample rubric.

After completing this session, participants will be able to:

- Describe rubrics and what questions they can answer.
- Describe the advantages of using rubrics.
- Describe the essential parts of a rubric.
- Distinguish between the various types of rubrics and determine when each is appropriate to use.
- Create their own rubric and apply it to their course(s).

• *Evaluating student learning in large classes: Designing the multiple-choice exam.* Large classes often necessitate using multiple-choice exams to assess student learning. However, instructors can find it challenging to write good items that ask students to do more than memorize facts and details. In this workshop we will explore how to create effective classroom multiple-choice exams based on sound learning objectives and how you can use information from your exams to improve your teaching.

After completing this session, participants will be able to:

- Describe various levels of learning objectives.
- Explain the strengths and weaknesses of multiple-choice exams.
- Identify common errors when writing multiple-choice items.
- Create multiple-choice items that assess various levels of learning.
- Use exam results for feedback and to evaluate instructional effectiveness.

• *Assessing your instruction.* In this workshop we will discuss the reasons for assessing instruction, the assessment process, integrating assessment into regular instruction, available assessment tools, and using assessment results. Specifically, workshop participants will be shown ways to integrate assessment into their instruction using the Ongoing Course Assessment (www.utexas.edu/academic/diia/oca/) system, the Course Instructor Survey (www.utexas.edu/academic/diia/assessment/course_instructor/), and the Division of Instructional Innovation and Assessment's Instructional

Assessment Resources Online (www.utexas.edu/academic/diia/assessment/iar/). Participants will have the opportunity to begin developing an assessment plan for a course.

After completing this session, participants will be able to:

- Explain the relationship between assessment and instructional best practices.
- Explain the assessment process.
- Understand three tools for assessing their instruction.
- Use assessment results to improve instruction and learning.
- Create an assessment plan for a course.

2. After attending the three core sessions associated with a particular series, students must also attend two elective sessions. These sessions may be culled from another series or they may be stand-alone electives. Examples of stand-alone sessions include time management and teaching in the diverse classroom.

3. When attendance requirements have been met, students have up to one academic year to submit an essay for certificate consideration. In the essay students must respond to the following question:

> Imagine that you have the opportunity to use the ideas you've learned from your core ASPECTS series to develop an assignment, lesson plan, or course plan in your field of study. Please select a minimum of one key idea from each of your three core ASPECTS sessions and describe how you would integrate these into an assignment, lesson plan, or course plan in your discipline. Use concrete examples to illustrate how these ideas from ASPECTS could be applied to your specific instructional setting or subject area.

4. Essay reviewers, who are also the session instructors, grade submissions based on the following rubric:

- **Almost always explains ideas using appropriate terminology.** Describes and integrates ideas from all three core sessions in a central thesis statement. Clearly connects the session concepts with classroom activities or plans, using three or more discipline-specific applications. Clearly articulates concrete examples that are very appropriate for the classroom setting and the discipline. Writing has clarity, coherency, and/or organization. Almost always uses proper grammar, spelling, and paragraph structure. Essay is the appropriate length. *Overall, the answer provides excellent examples, clearly shows connections between themes, and correctly demonstrates application to the student's discipline across all three core sessions.*

- **Frequently describes ideas using appropriate terminology.** Describes ideas from all three core sessions and integrates ideas from at least two core sessions in a central thesis statement. Connects the session concepts with classroom activities or plans, using at least two discipline-specific applications. Articulates concrete examples that are somewhat appropriate for the instructional context and discipline. Writing has clarity, coherency and/or organization. Almost always uses proper grammar, spelling, and paragraph structure. Essay is the appropriate length. *Overall, the answer provides relevant examples, provides some connections between themes, and demonstrates application to the student's discipline for at least two of the core sessions.*

- **Sometimes describes ideas using the appropriate terminology.** Mentions an idea from one or more sessions but only minimally integrates them. Connects the session concepts with classroom activities or plans, using at least one discipline-specific application. Uses examples that are vague or somewhat inappropriate for the instructional context and discipline. Writing has some problems with clarity, coherency, and/or organization. Sometimes uses proper grammar, spelling, and paragraph structure. Essay is either too long or too short. *Overall, the answer demonstrates basic comprehension of the material and its application to the student's discipline, but fails to provide adequate examples and show connections between themes.*

- **Rarely describes ideas using the appropriate terminology.** Mentions ideas from one or more sessions but does not integrate the ideas. Connects the session concepts with classroom activities or plans but fails to provide adequate discipline-specific applications. Uses examples that are vague or inappropriate for the instructional context and discipline. Writing often lacks clarity, coherency, and organization. Rarely uses proper grammar, spelling, and paragraph structure. Essay is either too long or too short. *Overall, the answer demonstrates some comprehension of the material,* *but fails to provide adequate examples, show connections between themes, or demonstrate application to the student's discipline.*

- **Almost never describes ideas using the appropriate terminology.** Mentions ideas from only one session. Does not connect the session concepts with classroom activities or plans, and fails to provide any discipline-specific applications. Makes little or no attempt to provide examples related to the instructional context and discipline. Writing consistently lacks clarity, coherency, and organization. Almost never uses proper grammar, spelling, and paragraph structure. Essay is either too long or too short. *Overall, the answer demonstrates very little comprehension of the material and fails to provide adequate examples or show connections.*

5. If students fail to receive a score of four or higher, they are provided feedback and may resubmit their essay for certificate consideration.

Variations

For additional information, please visit the ASPECTS web site at www.utexas.edu/academic/diia/gsi/aspects/.

Acknowledgments

The success of the ASPECTS program is a result of the efforts of many staff in the Division of Instructional Innovation and Assessment. In particular, I would like to acknowledge Dr. Lynn Jones Eaton, associate director for Faculty and Graduate Student Instructional Development, Dr. Dawn Zimmaro and Dr. Joel Heikes with Research, Evaluation, and Assessment, and especially Dr. Judy C. Ashcroft, dean of Continuing Innovative Education.

Mock Search Committee: Introduction to the Teaching Philosophy

Judith Gibber

Columbia University

GOALS
To provide insight into the criteria for a well-written teaching philosophy for an academic job search

PREPARATION TIME
- For instructor: 1 hour or more to search for and assemble appropriate teaching philosophies from the web
- For participants: About 1 hour of reading and thinking, at least one day before

EXECUTION TIME
20–30 minutes, if participants have read the philosophies in advance

RESOURCES
None

Introduction

When helping graduate students write a teaching philosophy for the academic job search, we usually start by providing trigger questions to encourage them to reflect on some aspect of their teaching. Answering these questions is difficult for graduate students because of their limited experience with teaching and their even more limited experience with teaching philosophies. They may also be hesitant to begin a workshop by sharing their personal thoughts about teaching.

Through the activity described here, students learn what makes a good teaching philosophy as they role-play members of a search committee trying to select the best candidate for a faculty position. As they read through candidates' teaching philosophies, they develop insight into what makes some more interesting than others, and they become more confident about their own ability to write a meaningful teaching philosophy.

Procedure

Before Class

1. Instructor assembles a collection of approximately six teaching philosophies that vary in content, organization, and writing style

and that have been posted on the web sites of faculty or graduate students at other institutions.

- If participants share a discipline, philosophies can be found by doing a web search for "teaching philosophy," "statement of teaching," or "teaching statement" with the name of the department.
- If participants are from across the disciplines, find approximately six representative examples from the natural sciences and from humanities and social sciences since writing and teaching styles vary greatly among these disciplines.

2. Remove the authors' names from the teaching philosophies and replace them with invented names (e.g., Astronomy Astrid or Sociology Sam).

3. Add a page where participants can summarize their responses to each philosophy, and include the following instructions:

> You are a member of a search committee that has received these six teaching philosophies as part of the application for a faculty position. As you read them, pay attention to the content, organization, and writing style. For each one, record:

- Features you especially liked
- Features you especially disliked
- Features you found especially memorable
- Questions you would like to ask this particular instructor
- Your recommendation for or against hiring this person

4. Distribute the philosophies and instructions for students to read.

In Class

1. Divide students into mock search committees of four to six students.

2. Give them about 15 minutes to share the notes they've jotted down about each teaching philosophy.

3. Reassemble as a group and ask participants to report on the features that they especially liked and disliked in the teaching philosophies. Create three lists on the board that summarize students' reactions. Responses from a recent workshop included these:
   - **Content:** *Liked:* Specific examples; mention of especially unusual or creative teaching activities; possible to visualize this person in the classroom; obvious that writer has teaching experience; men-

tions future plans, not only past experience; mentions how he developed as a teacher. *Disliked:* use of metaphors; saying "I'm enthusiastic" or "I have a sense of humor" without conveying that impression; long list of things he or she does in the classroom.

- **Organization:** *Liked:* clear organization; bullet points; use of white space, bold, italics to clarify organization.
- **Writing style:** *Liked:* short and concise; well written; able to hear the writer's voice. *Disliked:* starting all sentences with "I"; jargon. *Disagreed about:* formal or informal style.

4. Discuss the issues on which participants disagreed with each other. Point out that there will be similar disagreement within a real search committee. While it may not be possible to please all potential readers, one should try not to offend any of them.

5. This activity can be followed with the usual questions to stimulate students' thinking about teaching and a discussion about the first steps in writing a teaching philosophy.

Variations

1. Instead of providing real teaching philosophies, make up your own in which you vary the properties that you want students to note, such as length, vagueness, and use of jargon.

2. For one-time workshops, this activity can be done without advance preparation by students. Provide 20–30 minutes at the start of the workshop for participants to read the philosophies.

3. When using this technique in a class that consists of students from the same department, try to use teaching philosophies from faculty whom the students know. Remove the professors' names and ask the students to guess which professor wrote each. This task will illustrate how a teaching philosophy should reflect the individual instructor and not be a general philosophical discourse on effective instruction.

Teaching Portfolio Overview: Peer and Whole Group Discussion

Gabriele Bauer

University of Delaware

GOALS
- To introduce graduate TAs to the teaching portfolio process and elements
- To start graduate TAs purposefully collecting their own materials

PREPARATION TIME
Brief explanation prior to actual in-class activity

EXECUTION TIME
20–25 minutes, depending on the size of the TA group and the nature of the questions

RESOURCES
A handout adapted from materials by Seldin and Associates (1999) and Eison (1994), which follows this activity

Introduction

In preparing for their academic job search and the on-site interview process, graduate TAs are asked to document their teaching effectiveness, describe their teaching responsibilities, and indicate their teaching interests. The teaching portfolio offers an effective means to accomplish these tasks and provides a comprehensive, detailed, and evidence-based instructional portrait. In addition, the reflective work that students do in constructing their teaching portfolios prepares them to speak in an informed and confident manner about their teaching. Even when teaching portfolios are not requested as part of the application materials, their listing (or linking) on the candidate's curriculum vitae communicates to the search committee the candidate's scholarly approach to teaching. This activity provides a student-directed, reflective introduction to the portfolio process as well as a framework for focused reviews of sample portfolios.

Procedure

1. Distribution of teaching portfolio handout.
2. Individual reflection:
   - Students review the items (i.e., products of effective teaching, your own materials, and materials from others).

- Students circle existing items to include in their portfolio.
- Students star those items that may be available to them in the future.
- Students put a question mark next to those items that are unclear or that they would like to know more about.

3. Peer discussion:
  - Students turn to the person next to them and compare and discuss their findings.
  - Peers note commonalities/differences (brings in the disciplinary context) and decide on questions to discuss with the large group.

4. Whole group discussion:
  - Peers share their main observations and questions.
  - The instructor tracks salient aspects of the discussion on the board and uses the student observations and questions to contextualize and outline the portfolio process (e.g., What? Why? How?).

Variations

1. Whole group discussion is facilitated by peer teams and focuses on peer questions only.

2. Students receive the teaching portfolio handout prior to the class meeting and complete the individual reflection in preparation for the class discussion.

3. Students interview colleagues who are in the job market and/or junior faculty in their discipline about their experiences with developing and using portfolio materials. The handout serves as an interview guide either prior to or following the class meeting.

References

Eison, J. (1994, October). *Creating a teaching portfolio: The SCRIPT model.* Workshop session at the 19th annual meeting of the Professional and Organizational Development Network in Higher Education, Portland, OR.

Seldin, P., & Associates. (1999). *Changing practices in evaluating teaching: A practical guide to improved performance and promotion/tenure decisions.* Bolton, MA: Anker.

Creating Teaching Portfolios

The following are items that might be included in a teaching portfolio. The list represents a sampling of items to consider for inclusion depending on your particular teaching assignment, activities, and responsibilities. The portfolio materials included should make the best possible case for your teaching effectiveness.

Directions

Circle existing items to include in your teaching portfolio. Star those items that may be available to you in the future. Put a question mark next to those items that you would like to discuss further.

Products of Effective Teaching

Student test scores possibly before and after a course as evidence of learning.

Student essays, reports, creative work, projects.

Examples of graded student work along with TA's comments as to why they were so graded.

Student presentations on course-related work at on-campus conferences or events.

Evidence of help given to fellow TAs on teaching improvement (e.g., mentoring junior TAs).

Record of students who succeeded in advanced study in the field.

Testimonials from students or alumni about the TA's influence on their career choice.

Your Own Materials

Statement of teaching responsibilities.

Listing of course titles and numbers, credits, and enrollments with brief elaboration.

Reflective statement describing your personal teaching philosophy, learning objectives for students, and instructional strategies.

Representative course syllabus.

Description of course materials and tests prepared for students.

Information on your availability to students.

Information about direction/supervision of honors students, research group activities, or undergraduate student work in the lab.

Description of how multimedia, instructional technologies were used in your teaching.

Description of steps taken to evaluate and improve your teaching effectiveness (e.g., exchange course materials with fellow TAs, evaluate effectiveness of instructional innovation, participate in sessions to enhance teaching, participate in course development, contribute to professional journal on teaching your subject).

Material from Others (Students, Colleagues, Faculty, Chairperson, Others)
Student course and teaching evaluation data.

Written feedback (ideally unsolicited) from students, including letters, email messages after a course has been completed.

Honors received from students, such as a nomination for a TA Award.

Statements by faculty or faculty supervisors who have observed your teaching.

Statement by chairperson assessing your teaching contribution to the department, discussing how the department plans to use you as an instructor in the future.

PART TWO

ITA Development

CHAPTER **FOUR**

Culture

International teaching assistants (ITAs) can face special challenges when teaching for the first time in the American academy. The educational model used in most of the world calls for less interaction with instructors (the "experts") and more independent study from students. This top-down approach differs considerably from the lively interaction that is now considered best practice in American university classrooms.

For many ITAs, the topic of pedagogy is a relatively new one. While they may be aware of language issues, they may not have considered cross-cultural differences in teaching practice. The classroom is laden with pre-conceived and mostly unexamined notions of what constitutes "good" teaching. The task of identifying and making explicit the assumptions underlying one's pedagogy cannot be accomplished simply by telling people to teach a certain way. Rather, these assumptions must be unpacked and reflected on, added to and subtracted from, and refined every semester in order to succeed with American undergraduates, a diverse student body in every way imaginable: race, ethnicity, learning styles and learner developmental cycles (beginning learners vs. advanced learners, successful vs. struggling learners). Differences between the assumptions of ITAs and those of their students can lead to serious difficulties for everyone involved. We can mitigate these problems by engaging new ITAs in activities such as those presented in Chapter 4, which allow them to examine how culture shapes our pedagogical expectations and practices.

Cultural Adjustments

Barbara Gourlay

Brown University

GOALS
- To help ITAs develop a deeper understanding of the role culture plays in academic behavior
- To help ITAs improve their abilities to find similarities and differences in ideas and beliefs
- To help ITAs develop negotiating strategies in a conversational activity

PREPARATION TIME
None

EXECUTION TIME
30- to 90-minute class period

RESOURCES
Blank index cards

Introduction

Many ITAs struggle to adjust to teaching and learning in their new cultural context, where attitudes, priorities, and behaviors may differ from those to which they are accustomed. These international students frequently consider normal American undergraduate behaviors to be disrespectful, such as challenging a grade or questioning an instructor's statements or solutions in class. They must learn to interpret and handle these types of behaviors appropriately but seldom have the opportunity for this learning outside of the classroom. This activity provides ITAs with the chance to discuss some of the difficulties they may encounter in American academic culture. Through it, the participants learn to see behaviors in the context of larger cultural systems, rather than as independent positive or negative actions. For example, challenging a grade can be a behavior related to the larger American value of independent thinking or self-advocating. ITAs appreciate this activity to discuss cultural adjustment to the United States and to their new universities; at the same time they have the chance to practice summarizing, paraphrasing, and justifying a response, all critical skills for their success in the classroom.

Procedure

1. At the beginning of this activity, distribute one index card to each participant.

2. Ask each participant to write one aspect of American academic life that puzzles him or her. You may need to provide a prompt, such as, "If a friend were coming to study in the United States (or here at this university), what advice or warning would you give him or her before he or she arrived?"

3. Circulate and quickly review what each person has written and suggest modifications to grammar or expression as needed.

4. Elicit and list on the board some general categories that the students think their samples represent, such as student behavior, student attitudes, classroom procedures, and status of instructors.

5. In this 15- to 30-minute activity, each participant must find at least one person who has had a similar reaction to, or experience in, American classrooms. They then form a pair and seek other members to join their group. For example, two or more participants may decide that their shared category is best described as "test taking" and form a group based on this category. They can move around in groups, or they can move independently and form groups at the end.

6. Have ITAs use their cards only for reference and taking notes. All interactions must be verbal.

7. With the remaining class time, have the ITAs move into their self-appointed groups. A representative from each group explains how they classified or categorized themselves and why they formed the group that they did. If there is time, ITAs can also discuss why they did not form an alliance with another group. Remind the participants that there are no right or wrong answers, but they will need to justify their decisions in discussion.

Example from a Classroom Activity

Example of a Cultural Adjustment	Examples of Possible Categories for a Cultural Adjustment
Take-home exams are allowed.	Academic honesty or Tests
In China, teachers ask students to keep quiet in class while in the United States, teachers ask students to participate in class.	Classroom interactions or Teacher roles
Before every class, the professor asks students what has or has not been learned so the professor can adjust his or her teaching plan to be more suitable for all students. Sometimes though I have learned something in my undergraduate class, but I don't know how to express it in English. So I just say I don't know, and the whole class seems adjusted only for me!	Role of a teacher or Student preparation
Something odd about Americans is that they minimize physical contact. For example, when people wave—they don't shake hands or kiss each other; in the United States, only close friends do that. People wave to say hello and to say goodbye.	Greeting people or Rapport
There is almost no public transportation system here. You've got to have a car to survive.	Transportation or Essentials for survival
Students here sometimes have very casual behaviors in class. They wear slippers in the classroom. They put their feet on the chair. When they have questions about what the teacher says in class, they interrupt and ask the question immediately. And also, sometimes I think a few of them really do not care about the assignments.	Student behavior or Student work ethic
Another thing I still have not gotten used to is when people say "What's up?" or "How are you?" I know how to answer these kinds of questions. But the problem is when I meet the same people several times in one day and they keep asking me the same question.	Casual communication or Rapport
Generally American students ask lots of questions in class. They don't hesitate to stop the lecture to say "Say again."	Classroom interactions or Classroom management
When the teacher is teaching, he or she will often ask, "Are there any questions?" And he or she will wait for several seconds to see if there are any questions.	Classroom communication or Teacher behaviors
At night, people will say "Have a good night" rather than "Bye" or "See you."	Casual communication or Rapport
People are always nice. When they show their kind of welcome, I do not know how to carry on the dialogue—it's embarrassing.	Casual communication or Saving face

Diversity Awareness for ITAs

Doris Yaffe Shiffman

Johns Hopkins University

GOALS

To help prospective ITAs recognize the inappropriate ways they may unconsciously judge their students (e.g., by appearance, age, race, gender, ethnic heritage)

PREPARATION TIME

Time to look through several student newspapers and alumni magazines for 6–10 diverse photos of undergraduates

EXECUTION TIME

10–15 minutes

RESOURCES

Student newspapers and alumni magazines

Introduction

Although we teach our ITAs that we should not discriminate in the classroom on the basis of anything other than performance, it is helpful to inform ITAs about some unconscious prejudices that could enter into their interactions with undergraduates.

Procedure

Before Class

1. Peruse student newspapers and alumni magazines for pictures of undergraduates. Clip 6–10 colored pictures of a diverse group, such as heavy and slim students, students of different races and genders, students dressed in ways that announce an identity or that show something of significance (e.g., a student wearing a baseball cap and t-shirt with some humorous writing on it or a student carrying a violin case).

2. Place the photos on one sheet of paper and make enough copies so that no more than two students share a copy.

In Class

1. Hand out the photo sheets.

2. Ask students to imagine that it is the first meeting of the class they are teaching and that the undergraduates in the photos are those in the class.

3. The students should look at the photos and imagine that one undergraduate has caught their eye as someone who looks as though he or she would do well in the class.

4. Ask each student to state the number corresponding to the photo choice, and write those numbers on the board along with the count of how frequently each photo was chosen.

5. Tell students that they have the option not to respond, but if they choose that option, they should simply say, "I pass," without offering any additional comments.

6. After all the students have been surveyed, ask the class what was wrong with the experience. At this point expect some of the students to catch on, and then begin a discussion of how we should monitor ourselves so that we do not prejudge the undergraduates we teach on the basis of race, religion, ethnic origin, gender, nationality, appearance, disability, sexual orientation, or age.

High-Context Versus Low-Context Culture: Case Studies

Christine Liptak, Colleen Meyers,
Kyoung-Ah Nam, Elena Stetsenko
University of Minnesota

GOALS

- Students will be able to recognize significant cultural differences related to the importance of context/directness of communication (see handout that follows this activity) and analyze how those differences impact classroom communication.
- Students will gain practice giving a small group presentation to a large group.

PREPARATION TIME

30 minutes

EXECUTION TIME

One to two 50-minute class periods

RESOURCES

- Blank transparencies and transparency markers
- Copies of four case studies and questions for discussion
- Transparency of sample case study
- Copies of Think-Pair-Share handouts for pairs of students
- Copies of handout summarizing differences between cultures for each student

Introduction

The purpose of this activity is to help ITAs understand how their U.S. students perceive certain classroom behaviors, which may be different from how they perceive those behaviors in their own cultures, thus helping them relate to their U.S. students more effectively. Specifically, ITAs will look at these differences using case studies, each of which was adapted from an actual occurrence.

One caveat: Students may respond negatively to such a discussion should they feel they are being stereotyped or they may be in a state of denial (Bennett & Bennett, 2004) regarding cultural differences. However, we feel this topic needs to be covered in a safe environment. The instructor may want to begin with the following statement:

> Today, we'll be discussing cultural differences. We would like this to be an open and safe environment in which we can learn about each others' cultures—not only Asian versus Western but also Chinese

versus Turkish versus Korean. If anything is said that you find offensive or untrue, please feel free to speak up immediately. In addition, this lesson is not intended to overgeneralize; the purpose is to make you aware of what you might encounter.

Procedure

Before Class

1. ITAs can be given a brief article on high-context versus low-context cultures (e.g., information from the Peace Corps web site). We gave our ITAs the following pre-class assignment:

> Read the information on "Styles of Communication—Indirect and Direct" at www.peacecorps.gov/wws/publications/culture/pdf/workbook.pdf (page 78) and then answer the question below. Please be reflective in your answer. Short phrases or terse answers will not be accepted.

> *Question:* How would you compare your culture to U.S. culture with regard to directness (i.e., which culture is more direct/low context)? Differences in degrees of directness may create discomfort or even conflict. Give one example of what you've observed or predict what might happen in a classroom based on how your culture is different from U.S. culture.

In Class

1. Think-Pair-Share activity: Students work in pairs to brainstorm characteristics of high-context versus low-context cultures in terms of communication styles, using their homework responses as a guide. The instructor writes characteristics elicited from students on an OHP transparency.

2. The instructor distributes a handout summarizing differences in communication styles (following this activity) and asks students to compare their ideas with those on the handout.

3. The instructor explains the DIA model, described below, and applies the model to a specific classroom situation, which follows this activity.
   - *Describe:* What challenge do you see in this case study?
   - *Interpret:* Why do you think the ITA and the student feel or act

this way? What about each of their cultures (direct vs. indirect) may be underlying their feelings here? (Note that direct vs. indirect is only one component of high-context vs. low-context culture. Others include collectivism/individualism, saving face, harmony, etc.).

- *Analyze*: What could each person do or say to address the situation?

4. Group work: Students are divided into groups of four members, if possible from different cultures. Each group receives a case study of a situation that presents a classroom challenge. Group members analyze the case study using the DIA questions modeled in the previous exercise. A volunteer note-taker/summarizer writes the group's ideas on a blank transparency and is responsible for summarizing the case study during the group presentation. The other three group members each volunteer to present the group's answer to one of the three questions posed in the DIA model.

5. Group presentations: Each group of students goes to the front of the class to make their presentation. The note-taker summarizes (not reads!) the case study, and then each group member summarizes the group's response to the DIA question. Time is set aside for audience questions. The instructor can set a time limit for each group presentation (e.g., six minutes).

6. Debriefing: The instructor summarizes the activity by highlighting common themes and referring to the handout presented at the beginning of the class period. Be sure to save enough time for this part as the debriefing is one of the most important—if not the most important—part of the process.

Variations

1. If there is not enough time to finish the activity in one class period, students can get into their respective groups the following class period to review their content and briefly prepare for their presentation to the class.

2. If there's not enough time to do a pre-class assignment, Steps 1 and 2 can be omitted.

3. There is a scene from the film *Ferris Bueller's Day Off* (1986) in which Ben Stein portrays an economics teacher who bores his stu-

dents with the pseudo-interactive question, "Anyone? Anyone?" as he poses low-level fill-in-the blank questions related to "Voodoo Economics." ITAs can use the DIA model to analyze the students' reactions to his poor teaching, such as blowing bubble gum and sleeping.

References
Bennett, J. M., & Bennett, M. J. (2004). Developing intercultural sensitivity: An integrative approach to global and domestic diversity. In D. Landis, J. M. Bennett, & M. J. Bennett (Eds.), *Handbook of intercultural training* (3rd ed., pp. 147–165). Thousand Oaks, CA: Sage.

Hughes, J. (Writer/Director). (1986). *Ferris Bueller's day off* [Motion picture]. United States: Paramount Pictures

High-Context/Indirect Versus Low-Context/Direct Cultures

High-context cultures—rely on context (social or physical) to convey a large part of the message's meaning. Messages are more elliptical and indirect; don't trust words alone.

Low-context cultures—context is not assumed; messages are more direct and completely encoded in words; put thoughts into words and let them carry the meaning.

Think-Pair-Share Activity

In pairs, think of four to six comparative characteristics of high- and low-context cultures. List them in two columns. Be prepared to share your answers with the class.

High-Context Dimensions	Low-Context Dimensions
Indirectness: Tendency is to imply, say things indirectly. What is *not* said is important, making it even more important to pay attention to context (e.g., nonverbal communication).	*Directness:* Tendency to spell things out, be explicit and direct. Spoken words carry most of the meaning.

High-Context/Indirect and Low-Context/Direct Cultures
A Brief Overview

High-Context/Indirect Cultures	Low-Context Direct Cultures
Have been around a long time; have many rules, traditions, and protocols (e.g., Mexico, Middle East, Korea)	Are younger cultures or mixes of cultures (e.g., U.S., Australia, Israel)
Much common intuitive understanding (because of shared experiences)	Fewer shared experiences; less is taken for granted
Message often expressed not with words, but in what is *not* said or done or assumed by community members	Spoken words carry most of the meaning
Tendency is to infer, suggest, and imply; say things indirectly, circular	Tendency is to spell out things, be explicit and direct, linear
Live with more ambiguity	Tendency is to avoid uncertainty
More formal, everything "matters"	More informal, nothing matters, "anything goes" (e.g., California)

Compiled from:

Dodd, C. H. (1998). *Dynamics of intercultural communication* (5th ed.). New York, NY: McGraw-Hill.

Hall, E. T. (1989). *The dance of life: The other dimension of time.* New York, NY: Anchor Books.

Lanier, S. A. (2000). *Foreign to familiar: A guide to understanding hot— and cold—climate cultures.* Hagerstown, MD: McDougal.

Storti, C. (1999). *Figuring foreigners out: A practical guide.* Yarmouth, ME: Intercultural Press.

Case Studies: Low-Context Versus High-Context Situations

Instructions: There are four case studies below. Each base group will be given *one* case study to discuss. To discuss the case study, you should follow the DIA technique, listed here:

- *Describe:* What challenge do you see in this case study?

- *Interpret:* Why do you think the ITA and the student feel or act this way? That is, what about each of their cultures (direct vs. indirect) may be underlying their feelings here?

- *Analyze:* What could each person do or say to address the situation?

Case Study One: Handling Responses

Chen was teaching a class in his field. He wanted to make it interactive so he planned several questions. He asked the first question, and a student answered it. After she finished her response, he explained the concept to the rest of the class. The student then asked, "So, my answer was correct, right?" Chen was surprised that she hadn't realized her answer was correct.

Case Study Two: Second-Guessing the Question

Park is teaching a recitation. He finishes explaining a rather confusing concept when a student raises her hand. She starts asking her question but before she finishes it, Park responds by saying, "I know your question" and then re-explains the concept he was talking about in a different way. The student looks surprised. When he finishes his explanation the second time, he notices she is looking down and appears somewhat upset.

Case Study Three: Grading

Maria is a TA in history. She gave an assignment to her students that was worth a large percentage of their grade. Several students did the assignment and they got Bs. They came up to Maria after class and remarked, "Why did you give us a B? We've never gotten less than an A on an assignment like this before!"

Case Study Four: Instructor-Assistant Behavior

A U.S. professor is teaching an ESL class in which the students are taking a listening quiz. An assistant who is an undergraduate U.S. student is dictating the questions. During the middle of the quiz, the student looks at the professor and says, "I would never say it like this." The ESL students look up at the undergraduate TA and then at the professor, waiting for a response. The professor is shocked and doesn't know what to say. She thinks to herself, "Why didn't he say this privately to me instead of in the middle of the quiz?"

The High School Visit

Catherine Ross
University of Connecticut

GOALS

To give ITAs a clearer picture of the American high school and how freshmen students are prepared for and what they expect from college

PREPARATION TIME

1-hour PowerPoint presentation on American high schools (www.itap.uconn.edu)

EXECUTION TIME

2 hours for visit to a high school

RESOURCES

High school administrators or teachers willing to meet with ITAs, show them textbooks, and prepare a sample transcript that shows the average college-bound student's four years of coursework

Introduction

High schools in the United States differ markedly from those in most other countries. This difference is important for ITAs to understand because many of them teach introductory-level freshmen courses where they work with students fresh from the high school experience. One difference is that students who attend U.S. high schools are assigned to a particular school based on their home address. This means that students of very different backgrounds and academic levels but from the same geographical location are offered the same curriculum, which emphasizes breadth over depth. In contrast, many European and Asian countries have designated high schools not only to separate college-bound students from vocational students, but also to provide specialization for the college-bound students in areas like science, language, or the arts. A second major difference is that there is no one national standard for the U.S. high school curriculum, so in each state local school boards set the standards for their town, district, or county. The discussion of the differences between American high schools and the high school system in ITAs' home countries helps the ITAs realize that the freshmen they encounter in U.S. classrooms are very different from freshmen students in their home universities.

Procedure

1. The facilitator presents information (www.itap.uconn.edu) on American high schools, adding local information where applicable, and asks ITAs to discuss their initial reactions about what differences likely exist.

2. After the discussion the ITAs visit a local high school. Because this typically happens during the August pre-semester orientation, the high school may not be in session yet. If there are no students, vice principals may be willing to meet with the ITAs. *Optional:* The high school administrators (principal and/or vice principal) give the ITAs a tour of the high school, which for some ITAs is surprising due to physical facilities such as band or orchestra rooms, computer equipment, and science labs.

3. The ITAs meet in a central location, such as the cafeteria, where textbooks from various disciplines (chemistry, physics, calculus, algebra, geography, history, etc.) are displayed. The ITAs are invited to look through the textbooks, and they also receive a sample of a high school transcript for a typical college-bound student. About an hour should be allotted for questions and answers with the principals.

Variations

If an actual site visit is not possible, get copies of a sample college-bound student transcript to use in discussing differences during the PowerPoint presentation.

Interviews: Surveying College Undergraduates Who Attended High School in the United States

Margo Sampson, Vel Chesser, Stacey Lane Tice
Syracuse University

GOALS

- Overall, to promote natural communication with native speakers
- More specifically, to provide aural/oral skills practice and to learn what ITAs hear incorrectly or may not hear at all
- To provide an opportunity for ITAs to learn about the scholastic background of American students
- To provide an opportunity for ITAs to learn and practice idioms, follow-up questions, rejoinders, and active listening devices

PREPARATION TIME

In class:

- 15-minute introduction to activity three or four days before interviews start
- 15-minute practice session for asking questions—initial and follow-up
- 15-minute practice session on active listening, showing interest

EXECUTION TIME

Outside of class:

- Allow 2 months for ITAs to complete 12 ten-minute interviews

In class:

- 3 minutes for each final report; 5 minutes for written debriefing

RESOURCES

High school survey (which follows this activity)

Introduction

Because the ITAs who take our classes have little interaction with undergraduates, it is important to provide meaningful opportunities for them to communicate naturally with native speakers. This helps them learn about the culture and background of the undergraduates, which can have a positive impact on their teaching. Too often our ITAs tell us they speak English only in class—both ours and the ones they teach. We also find that they have a skewed idea of high school education in the United States. In addition to the cultural learning that takes place through the interviews, ITAs find that they can strike up conversations with undergraduates and that the undergraduates will usually cooperate willingly.

Procedure

1. ITAs should become familiar with the high school survey so they can look the person in the eye while interviewing.

2. They find someone on campus who is alone and appears not to be busy, then ask this person if he or she has 10 minutes to answer some questions about his or her high school experience.

3. The ITA take notes, but shouldn't forget to look at the person and show active listening.

4. After the interview, the ITA fills in the details on the interview sheet.

5. In class, the ITAs present the results of their surveys orally. Each presentation is about eight minutes.

6. In summary, each ITA notes five new and/or surprising facts he or she learned from the surveys, and then the class as a whole compares notes.

Variations

1. In addition to the survey, come up with two questions on your own.

2. Audiotape one of the interviews and transcribe it exactly (at least two pages).

3. Present your results in the classroom or the lab class.

4. Discuss interesting points with other undergraduates in casual conversation on your own.

High School Survey

Note to ENL 610 students: This survey is to be conducted orally. Do not let the undergraduates you interview write the answers themselves.

Year_____ Major_____

1. Where did you go to high school? _____

2. Was it public or private? _____

3. Were you in an honor's program?   Yes_____   No_____

4. Did you take Advanced Placement courses?   Yes_____   No_____

5. Did you take any other courses for college
   credit?   Yes_____   No_____

6. If you are from New York, did you receive a
   Regents diploma?   Yes_____   No_____

7. Which h.s. course was the hardest for you? _____

8. Which h.s. course was the easiest for you? _____

9. What kind of homework were you given? _____

10. What math courses did you take? _____

11. What science courses did you take? _____

12. How many hours per week did you spend doing homework? _____

13. Briefly describe the most *effective* teacher you had in high school.

    _____

    _____

14. Briefly describe the most *ineffective* teacher you had in high school.

    _____

    _____

15. What extracurricular activities did you participate in?

music_____   sports_____   yearbook_____

drama_____   language club_____

other (please list)_____

16. Did you work during the year in high school?   Yes_____   No_____

What kind of work did you do?_____

How many hours per week did you work?_____

17. What have you found to be the biggest adjustment from high school to college? _____

_____

_____

18. How do students usually pay for their college education? _____

_____

19. How much do students usually spend per semester on books? _____

_____

Please write your two questions (and the responses) on the back of this sheet.

CHAPTER **FIVE**

Pedagogy

Effective communication is key to academic success, whether in the classroom, the laboratory, department meetings, or conferences. International teaching assistants (ITAs) who speak English as a second language can be at a significant disadvantage when they begin teaching in the United States. They must adjust to a new pedagogical culture while they are simultaneously adjusting to communication conventions in American academic English.

American Teaching Performance

Pamela Pollock
Cornell University

GOALS

To study and practice the lecture style and communication strategies of American instructors (body language, gestures, eye contact), as well as to approximate their pronunciation, rhythm, and intonation patterns

PREPARATION TIME

None

EXECUTION TIME

5 minutes

RESOURCES

Recorded or live lectures

Introduction

This activity motivates students to combine listening, speaking, and non-verbal communication skills. It also allows students to consider lecture styles. It is particularly useful for helping students feel the rhythm and intonation patterns of English. Issues that arise in their teaching performances often initiate class discussions on various aspects of effective teaching. In addition, many ITA training courses require students to observe a class similar to one they might teach in the future. The American Teaching Performance could be one part of such an assignment. In any case, the student must get permission from the instructor they will observe and imitate.

Procedure

1. Students choose native English-speaking instructors from their own disciplines so that field-specific words and teaching styles are relevant. Give this assignment at least two weeks before the due date.

2. With the professor's permission, students record three to five minutes of a class lecture or seminar.

3. Students transcribe the recording verbatim and seek assistance with any unfamiliar vocabulary, expressions, or cultural information.

4. Students then mark the pausing, stress, linking, reduction, and intonation on the script, paying special attention to the word stress on the field-specific words. Careful listening is essential.

5. Students perform their mini-lectures in class, also trying to match the original gestures and body language.

6. Students' performances are recorded to allow them to analyze and compare their own and their professors' performances.

Movie-Based Activities for the ITA Course

Theresa L. Pettit

Cornell University

GOALS

- To practice suprasegmentals, gestures, idioms, and paralinguistic features of spoken English
- To examine examples of cross-cultural situations and teaching techniques

PREPARATION TIME

Varies

EXECUTION TIME

10–25 minutes per movie episode

RESOURCES

The following movies:

- *Lost in Translation* (2003)
- *Skyline* (1985)
- *The Mirror Has Two Faces* (1996)
- *Cheaters* (2000)

Introduction

ITA courses focus on building English proficiency through a framework that examines pedagogical, cross-cultural, and linguistic issues. All practice is contextualized and student centered. Because movies provide natural, nuance-filled language in culturally diverse contexts, they are a valuable instructional resource for presenting and reinforcing ITA program goals. The universal appeal of movies makes them a natural catalyst for practicing language. Because this medium offers excellent sources of both language and teaching samples, it is a powerful tool for use in ITA development courses.

Procedure

1. Before students are shown the video clip, they participate in a previewing activity, such as a discussion stemming from the general theme of the clip.

2. After the discussion, which is generally done in pairs to maximize the speaking time on task, the ITAs are shown the clip.

3. After they view the clip, students take part in post-viewing speaking activities.

4. Further language practice is encouraged through audio journal entries and language partner discussions.

Movie Clips and Activities

1. *The Mirror Has Two Faces*

   Discussion topic: Introduction to college teaching

   Clip locations: Three teaching scenes:
   - Gregory teaching at the start of the film (students are bored).
   - Gregory asking Rose to sit in on one of his classes and, subsequently, providing feedback to him (effective teaching strategies).
   - Rose teaching Gregory about baseball stats. Gregory teaches a class and students are more involved. Gregory thanks Rose.

   Pre-viewing activities:
   - In pairs, what are some adjectives that you would use to describe the teachers who greatly helped you to learn? Which adjectives would you attribute to those teachers who made it difficult for you to learn?
   - Large group debrief (written on OHP or board): What are the characteristics of effective teachers?

   Post-viewing activity:
   - How did Jeff Bridges's character change? What reaction did the students have? Identify the characteristics of effective teaching that Jeff demonstrated in the clip.

2. *Cheaters*

   Discussion topic: Academic integrity

   Clip location: After a teacher and his students obtain a copy of the upcoming academic decathlon exam, the teacher and students discuss whether it is right or wrong to use it to prepare.

   Pre-viewing activity:
   - From what you have read or heard, what are the policies regarding cheating and academic integrity at your institution? From your standpoint, what is the definition of academic integrity?

   Post-viewing activities:
   - What is your reaction to this clip?
   - What constitutes cheating? Provide examples of what you feel is cheating.

- What are your responsibilities as a TA regarding cheating?
- Role-play: One of you is a TA, and the other is a student who the TA believes was cheating on an exam. The TA's suspicions are confirmed by another student who admitted to seeing the student in question cheating.
  - ~ TA: You have asked a student to come to your office because you believe he or she cheated on an exam. Inform the student of your suspicions.
  - ~ Student: You have been called in by your TA and do not know why.

Variations

1. *Lost in Translation*
   Discussion topic: Culture shock
   Clip location: Opening scene
   Pre-viewing activity:
   - In pairs, describe how you each felt upon arriving in the United States. What caught your attention? Describe in detail what you were feeling and thinking.

   Post-viewing activities:
   - What do you think Bill Murray's character was experiencing as he entered Tokyo? Describe his emotions. Do you feel that he is beginning to experience culture shock?
   - What are the symptoms of culture shock? How does culture shock change as one stays in the country longer?
   - Tell a story about your experiences with culture shock. How have you or are you dealing with it?
   - What can be done to reduce the effects of culture shock?

2. *Skyline*
   Discussion topic: Difficult language situations
   Clip location: Elizabeth returns for the weekend
   Pre-viewing activity:
   - In pairs, describe a situation you experienced when there was a real breakdown in communication because of language.

   Post-viewing activities:
   - Do you think that Gustavo and Elizabeth share the same values?
   - Explain in detail why or why not.

- What could Elizabeth have done to help Gustavo through this difficult conversation?
- With your partner, role-play a situation you experienced in which you found yourself in a difficult language situation.

Sites with Movie-Based Activities Suitable for ITA Classes

1. allmoviescripts.com
   www.allmoviescripts.com
   Features hundreds of movie scripts.

2. American Rhetoric
   www.americanrhetoric.com
   Includes texts, photos, and sound bites from movie speeches. Excellent for practice with suprasegmentals.

3. antimoon.com
   www.antimoon.com/how/movies.htm
   Provides a rationale and strategies for watching movies as a method for improving English.

4. English, baby!
   www.EnglishBaby.com
   Features a conversation based on a recent movie followed by listening activities. An excellent site for listening comprehension activities.

5. English Teaching Forum Online
   http://exchanges.state.gov/forum/vols/vol38/no1/p24.htm
   Provides a lesson plan for working with videotaped programs, and more specifically, soap operas. The method described would also work well with movies.

6. ESL Cyberlinks
   www.james.rtsq.qc.ca/rreals2000.htm
   Most of the activities on this site are for reading and writing practice, but there are a couple of listening exercises based on movie clips that would provide good practice.

7. eslflow
   www.eslflow.com/Preind11speaking.html
   Provides more than a dozen links to other sites with movie-related activities. Sites feature how to use movies in class, grammar and vocabulary practice, proverb and idiom lessons, and worksheets. Some could be useful for follow-up practice.

8. esl-lounge.com
   www.esl-lounge.com/level2/lev2videojigsaw.shtml
   Features a tried-and-true activity called "Video Jigsaw." I saw it demonstrated using a *Friends* clip and have used it successfully several times, often with variations.

9. ESLnotes.com
   www.eslnotes.com/index.html
   Features plot summaries, exercises, and a glossary of vocabulary (slang, idioms, phrasal verbs, difficult vocabulary) in addition to cultural references.

10. ESL Partyland
    www.eslpartyland.com/students/nov/movies.htm
    Includes movie discussions, lessons, and handouts, as well as links to other sites with movie-based activities.

11. IATEFL Poland
    www.iatefl.org.pl/call/j_lesson16.htm
    This article by Marcin Jonik titled "Film Scripts Online" features lesson plans for *A Beautiful Mind* and *Shakespeare in Love.*

12. Internet Movie Database
    www.imdb.com
    Features movie trailers, message boards, movie recommendations, games, a glossary of movie terms, and plot summaries for thousands of movies. This site has endless possibilities for movie-based activities.

13. Internet TESL Journal
    http://iteslj.org/Lessons/Tatsuki-Movie/index.html
    Features ESL/EFL lessons using movies. Includes movie clips, activities, and handouts on various aspects of American culture.

14. Ohio University ESL
    www.ohiou.edu/esl/english/speaking.html#speakingactivities
    Features several links to sites that ITA trainers would find useful.

15. PowerSpeaking, Inc.
    www.powerspeaking.com/tip-49a.html
    These "e-tips" provide suggestions for using movie speeches to practice emphatic language. I highly recommend this whole website (www.powerspeaking.com) because it provides dozens of tips on how to become a more influential speaker.

16. Script-O-Rama
    www.script-o-rama.com/table.shtml
    Includes scripts from hundreds of movies. Excellent for creating exercises on stress, intonation, slang, phrasal verbs, idiomatic expressions, and other ITA course-related topics.

17. SimplyScripts
    www.simplyscripts.com
    Features hundreds of scripts from movies, television, and radio.

18. University of California, Berkeley
    http://teaching.berkeley.edu/bgd/diversity.html
    This article by Barbara Gross Davis titled "Diversity and Complexity in the Classroom: Considerations of Race, Ethnicity, and Gender" provides strategies for discussing and dealing with diversity issues in the classroom.

19. Virtual English Language Adviser Project
    http://vela.cs.ust.hk/demo/L4/
    Provides tips for developing listening ability while watching movies.

20. Writing Roleplays
    www.geocities.com/SoHo/Square/3472/sabrina.html#sabrina
    A step-by-step guide that provides information on how to construct lesson plans, and especially role-plays, from movies.

21. Yahoo! Movies and Film Trivia
    http://dir.yahoo.com/entertainment/Movies_and_Film/Trivia/Quizzes/
    Features movie quizzes that are great for follow-up class activities, discussion sessions, and audio journal tasks.

References

Colomo, F. (Writer/Director). (1985). *Skyline* [Motion picture]. Spain: Pacific Arts Video Records

Coppola, S. (Writer/Director). (2003). *Lost in translation* [Motion picture]. United States: Universal Studios

Stockwell, J. (Writer/Director). (2000). *Cheaters* [Motion picture]. United States: Home Box Office

Streisand, B. (Director). (1996). *The mirror has two faces* [Motion picture]. United States: Tristar Pictures

Pedagogical Uses of Critical Incidents Videos for ITAs

Stacey Lane Tice, Margo Sampson, Vel Chesser

Syracuse University

GOALS

- To provide practice in dealing with critical classroom situations that teachers frequently face
- To provide ITAs with opportunities to practice various speech acts such as apologizing, interrupting, asking for clarification, agreeing, and disagreeing

PREPARATION TIME

8-minute introduction to the activity

EXECUTION TIME

- Viewing each vignette: 2 minutes or less
- Writing a response: 5 minutes
- Discussing the responses and the changes: 10 minutes or longer if possible

RESOURCES

Critical Incidents in College Teaching videos
(http://gradschpdprograms.syr.edu/resources/problems.php)

Introduction

Training programs help ITAs with pronunciation, cultural information, and pedagogical strategies. However, in a classroom situation ITAs are often faced with issues that are difficult to handle on the spot because of a lack of experience. For example, when facing a cheating situation, ITAs must choose appropriate vocabulary, pronounce it clearly, and remain professional. Because we believe that practice in dealing with critical classroom situations teachers frequently face will help ITAs when or if the situations occur in their classrooms, we use critical incidents videos in our orientation programs.

Procedure

1. ITAs view a situation and then write about how they would handle it if it happened in one of their classes.
2. They then talk about it with other ITAs and TAs in combined groups.

3. Next they have a chance to decide whether they would make changes in their original responses to the situation. They present their rationale for changing or not changing to the group for further discussion. Interacting with native English-speaking TAs helps them with ideas, language/idioms, pronunciation, and so on.

Variations

1. Videos of critical incidents are also used in our classes where ITAs role-play, learn about gestures, and develop more facility with idioms and language.
2. Movies or parts of movies can also be used in place of the critical incidents.

Practice Identifying and Teaching to a Variety of Learning Styles

Anne Halbert

University of Connecticut

GOALS

- To increase the instruction of actual pedagogy in the ITA class
- To introduce the concept of learning styles
- To give the ITAs instruction in and practice of methods, strategies, and activities for their own teaching to support a variety of learning styles

PREPARATION TIME

Approximately 1.5 hours for the instructor to complete the learning styles questionnaire and read the accompanying information

EXECUTION TIME

Part of several class periods: 15 minutes for some classes, 30 minutes for others, an entire 1.5-hour class for the student presentations, depending on class size

RESOURCES

- Do an Internet search on "learning styles" for web sites that offer free learning styles assessments. Two are www.engr.ncsu.edu/learningstyles/ilsweb.html and www.learning-styles-online.com/ (this web site has courses and products for sale, but the assessment and explanatory information are free).
- Video recording and playback equipment if doing the variation involving videotaping the ITA presentations.

Introduction

The idea for this set of activities was sparked when an undergraduate assistant offering a way to improve the ITAs' explanation of a concept was heard to say, "It really helps me when the professor makes a chart." These activities give ITAs an opportunity to discover and reflect on both how they learn and how their learning processes or "learning styles" may be different from those of other students in the class. ITAs will also observe and identify teaching methods that support various ways of learning. Finally, the ITAs practice incorporating techniques and activities that teach to a variety of learning styles into their own teaching.

Procedure

In Class

1. Small groups comprised of ITAs and undergraduates discuss the question, "It helps me learn when the professor [does what]?"

2. Have a member of each group record the responses. (10–15 minutes)

3. The groups report their answers to the class and the instructor writes them on the board. (10 minutes)

4. The instructor collects the group responses and introduces the homework.

Homework (Undergraduates do this assignment as well)

1. Go to a web site with a free learning styles questionnaire and complete the questionnaire.

2. After getting the results, students should read the information provided about the different learning styles and write answers to the following questions:
   - What were the results from your questionnaire (your learning profile)?
   - According to the information on the web site, how do you learn best?
   - How does this compare with the activities/techniques you identified in class as helpful?
   - Think about the activities discussed in class and that you found on the web site. What set of activities that would support/be helpful to a variety of learning styles do you think you could incorporate into a class you will be teaching in your field?
   - What kind of advice would you give a student who asks, "How can I get an A in this class?"

In Class

1. Put the students into small groups with the undergraduates.

2. Students discuss the results of the questionnaires:
   - Do you think your profile is valid?
   - Did it surprise you in any way?
   - Did it confirm what you already knew about yourself? (10 minutes)

3. In the large group, the students report their learning profiles. (The instructor writes the information on the board along with the gender and major of the student to see if there are any patterns.)

4. As a class, discuss the fourth and fifth questions from the homework. (15–20 minutes)

5. The instructor collects the responses to the homework.

Homework

1. The ITAs observe a class or lab in their department.

2. They take notes on the activities/interactions in the class.

3. Students identify what learning styles the activities support and answer the following questions:
   - Are there any types of learners who might find the class difficult?
   - If yes, what types and what would be difficult for them?

In Class

1. As a large group, discuss what the ITAs observed:
   - Which activities do they think were successful?
   - Which ones do they think were not?
   - Were there things they observed that they'd like to do in their own classes?
   - Were there things they hope they never do? (10–15 minutes)

Homework

1. The ITAs prepare a short lesson that might be taught in an introductory class in their field, incorporating activities that support a variety of learning styles.

In Class

1. The ITAs teach the lesson they have prepared.

2. The class (instructor, undergraduates, fellow ITAs) write down activities, identify the targeted learning style(s), and give feedback on the activity's effectiveness. (15 minutes per student)

Variations

1. If your class does not have undergraduate assistants, separate the ITAs into groups of three or four.

2. In the small group discussions after the students have completed the learning styles assessments, the students could also discuss other questions about learning. For example: What is learning (i.e., strategic vs. deep)? What are the responsibilities of the teacher in the learning process? What are the responsibilities of the students?

3. Videotape the ITAs when they teach their prepared lesson and have them watch their videos for self-assessment with the instructor for feedback.

Preparing the ITA for Office Hours

Elizabeth Wittner

University of Virginia

GOALS

- To familiarize prospective ITAs with office hour protocol, procedures, and management
- To explore related cultural assumptions about TA and student roles
- To practice active listening, student-driven problem solving, and dealing with difficult interpersonal situations

PREPARATION TIME

Approximately 20 minutes to create index cards with problem scenarios

EXECUTION TIME

Approximately 90 minutes

ASSUMPTIONS

Undergraduate volunteers have been recruited to participate in the class session. Through previous readings and discussions, students have an understanding of the idea of teacher as facilitator and the difference between the transmission and construction of knowledge, as well as the strategies to foster independent student problem solving.

RESOURCES

- Undergraduate volunteers (at least one volunteer for every three students is ideal)
- Analytical problems (e.g., practice GRE problems, students' field-specific introductory-level problem sets, or textbook problem sets)
- Index cards, each with an "office hours problem situation"

Introduction

Holding office hours, a common duty for new TAs, can be a cultural minefield for international students who hold different assumptions about teaching and learning and who interpret behaviors differently from American students. Questions about grades, homework, and interpersonal issues may arise, and ITAs must be prepared to handle them. Their goal is to help the students in their sections or tutorials understand material, become independent problem solvers, and avoid relationships of dependency.

Bringing together American undergraduates with prospective ITAs can help build confidence, break down mutually negative stereotypes, and

foster understanding between the students and TAs. In post-session evaluations, both students and volunteers report that beyond the cultural
insights they gain, they also greatly enjoy the activity.

Procedure

Task 1: Write-Pair-Share

1. Prospective ITAs and undergraduate volunteers are asked to write
   for a few minutes about their own concerns, expectations, and positive and/or negative experiences with office hours.
2. Next, they divide into small mixed groups to discuss these themes
   from both student and ITA perspectives.
3. After about 10 minutes, a group spokesperson reports highlights
   back to the class as the instructor helps to draw out common
   themes.

Task 2: Role-Play Constructive Learning in Office Hours

1. Participants divide into small groups for an office hour role-play. In
   each group, one student plays the role of the ITA while the volunteer plays the role of an undergraduate coming to office hours for
   help with a problem set (the handout prepared in advance by the
   international students). The remaining student(s) in the group
   become active observers.
2. ITAs attempt to help their student with the problem set using skills
   they have learned previously, such as getting the student to think
   aloud, slow down, draw diagrams, and think systematically, rather
   than doing the homework problem *for* the student. The observer
   notes the quantity of work being done by the student as opposed to
   the ITA, taking note of such factors as who holds the pencil, who
   does most of the talking, and what happens when there is a mistake.
3. After about 10 minutes, participants discuss the experience from the
   perspectives of ITA, student, and observer, focusing on how effective
   the ITA was in helping the student and what he or she could do to
   be more effective.

Task 3: Role-Play Difficult Situations in Office Hours

1. Undergraduate volunteers and ITAs pair up to role-play an office
   hours scenario.

2. Each volunteer is given an index card that describes a difficult situation (e.g., *You are unhappy with the grade your TA gave you on your math exam and you want her to change it; You feel that the ITA's broken English is impeding your learning and you want to change sections; You don't think you're smart enough for this course; You want to ask the ITA to come to a party*).

3. The ITA does not see the card but tries to respond to the student accordingly.

4. Discussion after the role-play focuses on the cultural appropriateness of the TA's response and what is considered acceptable student/TA behavior at the university.

Variations

1. This activity could be split into various shorter lessons and extended over several weeks.

2. Volunteers could bring in actual homework if they are matched with a TA from their discipline.

3. Difficult scenarios from students' and volunteers' real-life experiences could be collected before the workshop to use for the role-plays.

CHAPTER **SIX**

Language

The techniques in Chapter 6 are designed to help international teaching assistants (ITAs) develop flexibility and accuracy in their interactions with students, whether in a recitation, a laboratory, or an office hour session. Within focused frameworks, these activities provide new instructors with the motivation to work on accurate articulation of discipline-specific vocabulary, build a repertoire of appropriate expressions to support effective pedagogy, and master the rhetorical strategies needed for successful classroom management.

Departmental Introduction Speech

Kimberly Kenyon
Cornell University

GOALS
- To have ITAs practice specific intonation functions in the context of a professional and persuasive speech related to their fields using paragraph-level discourse
- To have ITAs use discipline-specific keywords to work on the application of word and phrasal stress

PREPARATION TIME
20 minutes

EXECUTION TIME
Part 1: approximately 50 minutes
Part 2: approximately 45 minutes

ASSUMPTIONS
Students have learned some basic intonation contours for content words, emphasis, and thought groups.

RESOURCES
- Online departmental information about their field (e.g., www.chem.cornell.edu/grad and www.chem.cornell.edu/grad/concentration.asp)
- If available, online video about their field (e.g., www.chem.cornell.edu/grad/program video.asp)
- Reference text for further information about intonation

Introduction

This activity uses a departmental introduction speech to engage TAs in talking about their disciplines by having them act as departmental ambassadors for incoming students. In presenting the information about their fields of study, ITAs develop familiarity with the jargon of their disciplines. They also work on their comprehensibility in the areas of pronunciation, word stress (especially key terms in their fields), phrasal stress, and sentence stress.

Procedure

Part 1: Scripted Departmental Introduction

1. The instructor asks the ITAs to visit their departmental web site and copy a portion of the web site information to use as the frame for their departmental introduction. Each speech should be five to seven minutes and should include an overview of the program. Some areas of concentration for study should be mentioned so that ITAs get word stress practice with the real terms used to describe their field. (5 minutes)

2. The ITAs mark off the appropriate word stress, phrasal stress, and sentence stress for each sentence and review vocabulary. ITAs should include an introduction about themselves at the beginning of their speech. Students practice their scripted speech prior to performing the speech. (5–10 minutes)

3. ITAs are recorded giving the scripted departmental introduction, using the language from the web site as a script and practicing the intonation patterns, speaking to the rest of the class who act as the new graduate students in their department. (5–7 minutes)

4. The instructor reviews the video with each ITA and points out areas for language improvement, or posts the video online for ITA self-review. In doing the self-review, the ITA reviews the video with attention to areas for improvement and works on an audio journal to redo the parts needing work. The instructor debriefs the ITA in either a one-on-one conference or via written or recorded feedback on the speech. (20–30 minutes)

Part 2: Impromptu Departmental Introduction

1. Students in class are paired up to discuss what is really important to know as a graduate student in their department. Students brainstorm important information and ask clarifying questions about one another's fields, majors offered, types of facilities, research opportunities, advisement, policies for graduation, and so on. As departmental representatives, they can also address the question, "What advice would you give new students that isn't on the departmental web site?" (5–7 minutes)

2. Based on their brainstorming, students individually consider what will be included in their departmental introduction. They will have

seven minutes each to address the new members of their department. Their presentations should be comprehensible and clear. (2 minutes)

3. ITAs are recorded giving an impromptu departmental introduction speech. (7 minutes)

4. ITAs view both the scripted and the impromptu recordings online and compare and contrast the language in both speeches in their audio journals. They redo the impromptu speech with attention to the areas they believe need improvement. Their instructor debriefs them in conference or via feedback on the impromptu speech. (20–30 minutes)

Variations

1. Do only Part 1 or Part 2.

2. Have the ITAs introduce their fields to undergraduates in their departments.

Developing Oral Communication Skills

Margaret Lawrence

University of Washington

GOALS

By the end of this workshop, participants should be able to:
- Identify techniques and resources for working on improving their English.
- Identify the key features of stress and rhythm in English and model them.
- Define *collocation* in a general sense, explain its importance to language learning, and identify collocations in a sample text.
- Identify a few key features of "fast speech."

PREPARATION TIME

- For workshop leaders, a minimum of one to two hours to assemble any necessary resources, depending largely on the previous experience of the leader and the availability of materials
- For workshop participants, no previous preparation

EXECUTION TIME

75 minutes

RESOURCES

- A three- to four-minute clip of a video or DVD of a class discussion (featuring U.S. students) in which students with a variety of discourse styles are participating
- Several overhead transparencies or handouts:
  - ~ A limerick for rhythm practice
  - ~ A collocation "test" consisting of four or five sentences, each with a blank substituted for a missing word or phrase. The blank should represent a collocation in that only one or at most two or three words or expressions can legitimately fill the blank (e.g., "His ex-wife claims he has never _____ his responsibilities to his children because he has not paid enough child support").
  - ~ A text excerpt from *Newsweek* or other collocation-rich resource
  - ~ A transcript from previously mentioned video clip of class discussion

Introduction

The audience for the voluntary ITA-specific workshop described here ranges in size from 20–35 participants from a wide variety of disciplinary backgrounds, more than half of whom have had less than one year of formal teaching experience. The Communicating in American English workshop presents different strategies for ITAs to use in developing their oral communication skills in English.

Procedure

1. Introduction: Explain the purpose and goals of workshop. (2 minutes)

2. Ask participants to form groups and discuss what concerns they might have about teaching in English. (3 minutes)

3. Discuss these concerns and give quick tips and reassurances. (5–7 minutes)

4. Ask participants to brainstorm helpful resources and strategies for improving English on their own. Write their suggestions on the overhead and add your own tips. Pass out handouts of tips and resources. Transition to teaching and practicing several particularly key aspects of English: rhythm and stress, collocations, and listening to fast speech. (12 minutes)

5. Rhythm and stress: Write a multisyllabic word on the overhead, and ask participants which syllable is stressed. Ask what differentiates stressed and unstressed syllables, and then discuss length and pitch. Write a sentence on the overhead and read it aloud. Ask which words are stressed, and then explain sentence stress, content and function words, and stress timing with more examples. Have participants practice briefly with examples as you explain. Finish by having them practice with a limerick shown on an overhead or in a handout. (12 minutes)

6. Collocation: Explain the basic idea of collocation. Put a collocation "test" on an overhead and give participants five minutes to try to figure out which words go in the blanks. Go over the "test" and explain. Put a text excerpt from *Newsweek* on the overhead and ask students to identify all collocations as you go through the text. Encourage them to identify and collect useful collocations as they read or listen to English during their ordinary routines. (20 minutes)

7. Listening to fast speech: Quickly ask several students "didjaeatyet?" ("Did you eat yet?"). Usually no one can understand the question. Occasionally one student understands. Explain reductions and assimilation with some typical examples. Reassure student that usually fast speech is easier to understand than "didjaeatyet?". Talk

about "filler" language and how that can also distract a nonnative listener from catching the main idea of a speaker. Also discuss how U.S. students' speech may be hard to understand at times because students may use fragmented English if they are struggling to express themselves. Give some background for student discussion on the videotape clip and then ask participants to identify the speakers' main ideas while you play the tape. Go over the transcript and point out and discuss features of student speech. (20 minutes)

8. Summarize major themes. (1 minute)

Discovering and Teaching the Vocabulary of the Academic Communities

Doris Yaffe Shiffman

Johns Hopkins University

GOALS

- To introduce ITAs to language specific to their universities and to language common to U.S. college life in general
- To introduce ITAs to features of undergraduate life

PREPARATION TIME

1–3 hours to read through the first published student newspaper of the academic year or to find other sources of this type of vocabulary, and to prepare a vocabulary list for the class activity

EXECUTION TIME

5 minutes during one class and one subsequent 50-minute classroom period

RESOURCES

The first undergraduate student newspaper of the academic year and either its web site or enough copies to hand out to each ITA

Introduction

Each September the student newspaper of Johns Hopkins University has an orientation edition to help freshmen adjust to the university and surrounding community. This edition always includes one article about language unique to Johns Hopkins. For example, the fall 2005 edition included an article titled "More Jargon Than You Can Throw a Freshman at: Learning JHU Lingo" (media.www.jhunewsletter.com/media/storage/paper932/news/2005/09/09/CampusLife/More-Jargon.Than.You.Can.Throw.A.Freshman.At.Learning.Jhu.Lingo-2243246.shtml).

The article contains some discussion of the terms, although it is written more to amuse readers than to clearly explain the phrases chosen. Included among the jargon specific to Johns Hopkins are such phrases as *Arts and Crafts* (the name engineering students give to the school of arts and sciences), *AMRs* (the freshmen dorms), and *CollTownShuttle* (the bus that takes students to the train station and the medical school campus) as well as other terms often familiar to students at any university, such as *AcPro, premed,* and *orgo.* As each term is defined, other slang words common to U.S. universities, such as *frats, geeks,* and *cutthroats* are used and offer students additional opportunities to interact with the language of college campuses. An introduction to this kind of vocabulary can be enormously useful as ITAs develop the small-talk skills that make office hours and other encounters with students outside of class comfortable.

Procedure

Before Class

1. Look through the academic year's first edition of the undergraduate newspaper for an article about slang terms or general vocabulary specific to your university. If no such article exists, look for such terms throughout the paper.

2. Create a list of the terms you would like students to learn. If the terms are from a specific article about campus language, then you may only need to indicate where the article can be found. If they have been chosen from various articles in the paper, write beside each word the name of the article and the page and paragraph number in which it can be found.

Class 1

1. Hand out the list of terms and assign each student three to four words (depending on the number of vocabulary items and the number of students in the class).

2. Request that students not use a dictionary to ascertain the meaning but instead ask an undergraduate for help or try to come up with a definition from the context and to bring that information to the next class.

Class 2

1. Divide the ITAs into working groups of three to share and fine-tune the definitions/explanations for the terms they have each been assigned.

2. Reassemble as a large group. Suggest that each student look over the words not assigned to his or her working group to identify which words from the rest of the list are unfamiliar to them. Then ask the students who researched those words to share with the entire class the definitions they came up with.

3. Finish the session discussing how the campus culture revealed in the vocabulary list differs from that of the ITAs' undergraduate cultures.

Editorial Jigsaw

Barbara Gourlay
Brown University

GOALS

- To develop ITAs' skills in providing oral summaries and reporting information
- To expand ITAs' English vocabulary and familiarity with common English idioms
- To increase ITAs' knowledge of the local academic community to foster comfortable conversation outside of the classroom

PREPARATION TIME

10–30 minutes

EXECUTION TIME

50–75 minutes

RESOURCES

Campus newspaper

Introduction

The ability to briefly summarize and report information is a valuable skill for ITAs to demonstrate. In classrooms and in office hours, ITAs are frequently required to provide summaries of what has been discussed, asked, or presented during class. ITAs also need a certain level of familiarity with the events and activities of the local academic community to use when engaging in small talk with their students before or after class. In many cases, familiarity with the local academic community allows for more efficient explanations of concepts. For example, in economics classes, ITAs can incorporate references to campus events or activities familiar to undergraduates when explaining economic concepts.

This activity uses a Jigsaw exercise format to work on two skills: summarizing information and gaining familiarity with the local community. ITAs enjoy the opportunity to explore current topics of local interest. Subsequently, these graduate students have a good supply of small talk to use in interactions with undergraduates.

Procedure

1. Before class, select three to five recent editorials from the campus newspaper, and make enough copies so that each member of a group has a copy to make notes on.

2. In class, divide the students into groups of three or four students, depending on the class size, as follows:
Group A: A1, A2, A3
Group B: B1, B2, B3
Group C: C1, C2, C3

3. Assign one editorial to each group, and give each member a copy of the editorial.

4. Provide 5–10 minutes for the group to read the editorial and consult with each other about its vocabulary and message.

5. Provide the groups another 10 minutes to summarize the main information in their editorials. Encourage ITAs to take notes to help them with the next part of the exercise.

6. As in a typical Jigsaw exercise, regroup the ITAs. The new groups will have one representative from each of the previous groups. All members of the new groups will have read different editorials:
New Group 1: A1, B1, C1
New Group 2: A2, B2, C2
New Group 3: A3, B3, C3

7. The ITAs take turns sharing the information from their editorials by summarizing the main ideas for the other members of their new groups. This takes about 30 minutes.

8. At the end of the session, the class can discuss questions or concerns about the editorials.

9. Encourage ITAs to talk with people outside of class about the issues from the editorials. At the next class, they can report on those out-of-class discussions.

Variations

This exercise can focus on a particular topic. For example, if ITAs are unfamiliar with certain university procedures or policies, such as grading policies or plagiarism, the source material can come from university or departmental publications. If you have a long text you want ITAs to work with, then a longer passage can be divided into smaller sections and assigned to groups. Using this approach, all ITAs can become familiar with the information in the entire passage by discussing it in an interactive and collaborative way.

Fielding Questions: The IgNobel Prizes

Barbara Thompson
Princeton University

GOALS

To provide practice in fielding questions, restating them, and answering in a direct manner

PREPARATION TIME

15 minutes or less

EXECUTION TIME

10 minutes for students to prepare what they want to say, and then 3–5 minutes per student

ASSUMPTIONS

Students have been introduced to the skills of negotiating questions, restating them, and responding to them appropriately.

RESOURCES

A list of IgNoble Prize winners, which can be downloaded from the Internet and duplicated for the students

Introduction

One of the most important skills for ITAs to develop is the ability to field questions. This exercise allows students to practice question-handling in an enjoyable context. The IgNobel Prizes, a spoof on the Nobel Prizes, are awarded annually to 10 researchers for papers that are authentic, amusing, and thought provoking. One typical example is the research that found that chickens prefer beautiful people. At the ceremony at Harvard University, most of the prize winners are present to accept their awards, give a short speech, and enjoy laughing at themselves.

Procedure

1. Following a brief discussion to describe the IgNobel Awards, the instructor distributes a list of titles of some of the award-winning research papers. This activity is always most successful when only the funniest ones are on the list.

2. Students must choose one of them and prepare a two-minute acceptance speech in which they talk about the research project.

3. Pretending to be the award-winning scientists, the students deliver their acceptance speeches and field questions about their research from the audience.

4. The student who is presenting must respond to the questions using the techniques discussed in class previously. If they don't understand the question, they must negotiate the meaning with the person who asked it, then restate the question, and finally respond directly and fully.

The Fine Art of Q&A

Barbara Gourlay
Brown University

GOALS
To help ITAs develop comfort, fluency, and accuracy in question/answer interactions typical of American classrooms

PREPARATION TIME
The time it takes to create index cards with question commands

EXECUTION TIME
Variable as a supplement to presentation practice or discussion practice

RESOURCES
None

Introduction

For many international students, the classroom interactions that characterize higher education in the United States present a significant challenge. These students are accustomed to educational environments where instructors focus less on fostering interaction and more on direct delivery of course content.

This activity is designed to help international students, early in the semester, develop fluency and comfort with question/answer interactions. In an ITA preparation class, the use of index cards with assigned questions encourages participants to interrupt the presenter politely with a question. At the same time, these interruptions provide the presenter with more opportunities to practice fielding questions generated by the class members. The result is that all members of the class are productively engaged in the activity and in developing the skills necessary for success in interactive classrooms. After several sessions at the start of the term, the cards are no longer necessary prompts. By this time, students are more comfortable with interactive communication tasks.

Procedure

1. Before the class, create an index card for each participant. Each card will contain one of the following prompts:
   - Ask a *who* question.

- Ask a *what* question.
- Ask a *where* question.
- Ask a *when* question.
- Ask a *why* question.
- Ask a *how* question.
- Ask a *yes/no* question.
- Ask *any* question.

2. Distribute a card to each student with instructions to complete the task on the assigned card at some point during the class period. Participants must ask the assigned type of question but may ask other questions as well.

3. The class format and context in which students ask their assigned types of questions can vary from instructor-led explanations to peer impromptus, formal presentations, and small group work. Discussion and assessment of students' production, in terms of vocabulary, grammar, and appropriateness, can be treated individually or in a more general debriefing session following the activity.

4. Depending on the instructor's pedagogical goals, the cards can encourage participants to:
   - Attend to accuracy in forming questions
   - Be direct and concise
   - Develop a repertoire of appropriate expressions for interruption and resumption of speech
   - Learn how to buy time when formulating and framing answers

The Greek Alphabet: Speaking in Symbols

Barbara Gourlay

Brown University

GOALS

- To help ITAs develop clear articulation of common discipline-specific formulas and expressions involving the Greek alphabet
- To help ITAs develop skills at monitoring production and self-correction
- To help ITAs establish contacts of content-area specialists who can model the expressions

PREPARATION TIME

None

EXECUTION TIME

50 minutes

RESOURCES

Worksheet on Greek Alphabetic Practice (following this activity)

Introduction

Many fields use symbolic language that includes letters from the Greek alphabet. Knowing how to express equations in spoken English can be a challenge. For example, new international students may understand what A B means, yet they may struggle when articulating "A is true if and only if B is true" in spoken language. In addition, the English pronunciation of many symbols may be unfamiliar to new international students. Articulating the "l" in *Alpha* or *Delta* and the "th" in *Theta*, for example, can be challenging for many ITAs. This worksheet activity is designed to motivate ITAs to accurately express meaningful symbols that they recognize as important in their academic discourse. In the process of completing this worksheet, ITAs may establish peer consultants in their home departments as content-area resources to help with the accurate expression of symbolic language.

Procedure

1. Distribute the worksheet and ask the ITAs to complete the column labeled "In-Context Example" at least one day before the pronunciation workshop session. (The worksheet provided here has been mod-

ified to fit onto one page. Note that ITAs usually need more space to write their formulas and expressions.)

2. Conduct a workshop in which the ITAs share their in-context examples of symbolic language in one of the following ways, depending on the group size:
   - In rotating pairs
   - In small groups
   - One at a time using the board or overhead
   - In individual consultations

3. Direct students to take notes that apply to their pronunciation problems in the "Pronunciation Notes" section of the worksheet.

4. Because disciplines vary in their expression and pronunciation of symbolic language, an information exchange may inspire debate about proper expression. If no consensus is possible, the ITA who brought the expression to class must consult with a trustworthy departmental source to confirm the appropriate expression and pronunciation. In the following class session, the ITA reports back with the "expert testimony."

Greek Alphabet Practice

Name_____

Department_____

Greek Letter	Symbol	Pronunciation Notes	In-Context Example from the Discipline	Additional Examples
Alpha	α, A			
Beta	β, B			
Gamma	γ, Γ			
Delta	δ, Δ			
Epsilon	ε, E			
Zeta	ζ, Z			
Eta	η, H			
Theta	θ, Θ			
Iota	ι, I			
Kappa	κ, K			
Lambda	λ, Λ			
Mu	μ, M			
Nu	ν, N			
Xi	ξ, Ξ			
Omicron	o, O			
Pi	π, Π			
Rho	ρ, P			
Sigma	σ, Σ			
Tau	τ, T			
Upsilon	υ, Y			
Phi	ϕ, Φ			
Chi	χ, X			
Psi	ψ, Ψ			
Omega	ω, Ω			

"International Teaching Assistant of the Year" Speech

Kimberly Kenyon

Cornell University

GOALS

- To have ITAs practice narration and description in context by creating an engaging commencement speech that targets storytelling
- To improve tense control in the three major time frames and the ability to foreground important information and background less important information

PREPARATION TIME

The time needed to become familiar with the commencement speech sample

EXECUTION TIME

Approximately 60 minutes

ASSUMPTIONS

ITAs have already reviewed storytelling and understand that they should have a beginning, middle, and end, with transitions between ideas and a sequence of events chronologically ordered.

RESOURCES

- The text and audio of a speech that includes stories (e.g., Steve Jobs's commencement speech [http://news-service.stanford.edu/news/2005/june15/jobs-061505 and audio: www.stanford.edu/dept/news/report/news/2005/june15/videos/53.html])
- Reference text for further information about intonation

Introduction

ITAs need to develop the ability to use narration and description, as well as to control other aspects of language such as time frames. In fact, ITAs may be more likely to build rapport with their students and interest them in their field if they can share personal experiences with them.

Procedure

Before Class

1. For homework, ITAs listen to one of the stories from Steve Jobs's commencement speech (www.stanford.edu/dept/news/report/news/2005/june15/videos/53.html). They can also use the text if needed (http://news-service.stanford.edu/news/2005/june15/jobs-061505). In their audio journal they should paraphrase the part of the speech

they listened to and discuss how Steve Jobs's used stories and transitions in his speech. (10–15 minutes)

In Class

1. In class, the ITAs are paired to discuss what is really effective about using stories to express themselves. They brainstorm and tell stories from their past using these general ideas:
   • A story from your past and its impact on you in the past, present, and future.
   • A story about an inspirational teaching or learning moment from your past, how it impacted you as a teacher, and how it will impact your future students.
   • A story about a teaching difficulty in the past that was motivating or frustrating, how that experience molded your teaching, and what it has done for you as a teacher. (7 minutes)

2. ITAs have two minutes to prepare to use one or more of the ideas from Step 1 to give a three-minute impromptu "ITA of the Year" speech.

3. ITAs take turns giving their speeches. (3 minutes per student)

4. The instructor and/or undergraduates ask clarifying questions about the story and give feedback on the target language foci of the speech. (2 minutes per student)

5. ITAs have two minutes to prepare a longer (seven-minute) impromptu "ITA of the Year" speech that introduces who they are, uses one or more of the ideas in Step 1, and pulls in other information such as:
   • Their teaching philosophy
   • A description of courses and duties
   • Innovative instructional techniques and contributions
   • Contributions to instruction above and beyond the call of duty
   • Contributions to instruction outside of the classroom
   • Self-improvement efforts regarding teaching

6. Students are videotaped giving their impromptu "ITA of the Year" speeches. Students are allowed to use notes because this is not a memorized speech, but it should also not be considered a reading exercise.

7. The instructor posts the speeches online for ITA review. Each ITA reviews the video with attention to areas for improvement and works on an audio journal to redo the areas needing work. The instructor debriefs with them in a one-on-one conference or via written or audio-recorded feedback on the speech. (15–20 minutes).

Variations

1. The ITAs practice Steve Jobs's speech by marking the intonation pattern and practicing the speech in their audio journal.

2. The ITAs prepare their speeches ahead of time and use the exercise to practice intonation and pronunciation.

Mimicking American TA Discourse

University of California–Los Angeles

GOALS
To practice speech patterns by mimicking American TA discourse

PREPARATION TIME
Obtain an audio segment of an effective American TA teaching a class. Usually 30–60 seconds of speech is sufficient for this activity.

EXECUTION TIME
20–30 minutes of presentation; 20 minutes for feedback

ASSUMPTIONS
Participants will have had a basic introduction to the role of suprasegmental discourse features in English.

RESOURCES
- Recording of 30-60 seconds of an effective American TA in class (any format: cassette, CD, DVD, video, or digitized sound file)
- Playback equipment in class
- A written transcript of the speech segment on an overhead transparency with a font size of at least 18
- Recorded segment posted on course web site

Introduction

This activity targets high-priority speech features for students to practice using recorded segments from a class taught by an American TA. Such features include thought groups, stress, intonation, linking, focus words, and reduced speech. Virtually any segment of speech you select will contain all of these features. If the plan is to study more narrowly defined speech features, for example intonation in questions, the instructor will need more time to find a recorded interactive segment that includes multiple questions. Students 1) listen intensively to a relatively short segment of speech, 2) analyze it for the target feature, and 3) imitate the speech by recording the transcript and comparing their versions with the original.

Procedure

In Class

1. Choose and review one target feature and its role in verbal communication, including a summary of related research, if desired.

2. Give students a transcript of the selected 30- to 60-second speech segment and have them predict how the target speech feature might occur in this excerpt. For example, students can mark where they anticipate that pauses between thought groups might occur.

3. Paired students compare their marked-up copies of the transcript.

4. Viewing the overhead transparency of the transcript, students discuss the patterns that they anticipated for the feature under discussion.

Homework

1. Students watch/listen to the segment of recorded speech on the course web site and check the predictions that they marked on their transcripts against the real speech.

2. Students then reproduce and record the speech segment in a sound file.

3. They listen to the sound file, compare their discourse with the original, and submit a brief written evaluation of their performance.

Practicing Communication Strategies

Doris Yaffe Shiffman
Johns Hopkins University

GOALS

- To introduce prospective ITAs to the importance of nonverbal communication
- For ITAs to practice various communication strategies in a controlled environment where their attention is not focused on the content of the presentation

PREPARATION TIME

15–20 minutes to choose questions from the book *Talk about Trivia: 1001 Questions*, or 2 to 3 hours to create one's own questions

EXECUTION TIME

Two 50-minute class periods

RESOURCES

Multiple-choice questions about North American culture either written by the instructor or chosen from a book, such as *Talk about Trivia* (Schoenberg, 1986)

Introduction

Before ITAs do their first practice teaching, it can be helpful for them to practice effective communication strategies, such as nonverbal communication, without having to prepare an extended teaching sample. One technique is to have students form teams, then give each student a multiple-choice question about American culture (without the answer) to ask his or her teammates. Sample questions include:

1. From *Talk about Trivia:*

    A strike is always good for _____.

    baseball players

    bowlers

    workers

2. Created by the instructor:

    Which of the following museums is not located on Baltimore's Inner Harbor:

    The Walters Art Museum

The National Aquarium in Baltimore

The Maryland Science Center

Procedure

Before Class

1. Select the communication strategies you would like the students to practice (e.g., volume, rate of speech and pausing, movement, gestures, eye contact, friendliness, emphasis, and board use).

2. Decide which features you will emphasize and in what order. (The order can vary, but it is best to end with board use since it is the only technique ITAs can practice without needing to concentrate on speaking clearly, too.)

In Class

1. Divide the class into two teams.

2. In a class with an odd number of students, invite one student to be the judge of the communication strategies instead of belonging to a team. If the class number is even, it is possible to have two judges who confer or take turns before they allocate points.

3. Before each round of questions, introduce a new strategy and explain how the ITAs should use it in their teaching to make their communication more effective.

4. After each explanation, a member of each team should go to the front of the class and ask teammates a question selected by the instructor while also demonstrating the newly explained strategy and making use of the ones already discussed.

5. Rules of the game:
   - For the first question, the team gets one point if the ITA successfully employs the new skill and a second point if the team gets the answer correct.
   - For the second round of questions, a new ITA from each team asks a question. It is possible for each team to gain three points, one for the correct answer, one for the previously demonstrated skill, and one for the new skill.
   - For successive questions, the team still gets a point for a correct answer and one if the ITA makes use of the new skill, but the

third point is divided into fractions which add up to one point, and the team gets a percentage of that point, depending on how many skills have been introduced and how successful the ITA is in employing each of the ones discussed up until then.

- The ITA cannot suggest to the group what he or she thinks the answer might be. Instead the team members have 30 seconds to answer. If they are unsure of the question, they may ask to hear the question one more time and they again have 30 seconds to offer a response.
- If an ITA needs to ask a question twice (and this almost always happens), only the way the question is asked the second time counts toward points for the strategies.

6. After each question has been answered by the team, the instructor supplies the correct answer and the appointed judge or judges from the class determine how many points each ITA receives for his or her practice. The instructor also gives feedback on how effectively each ITA employed each previously discussed strategy.

Variations

Students may become so absorbed in the game that they forget to employ the communication strategies, just as they might during their actual teaching. One way to make the ITAs more aware of how they are succeeding and to give them an opportunity to improve is for the instructor or the student judge to stop the game after a question has been asked for the first time and briefly discuss what strategies the ITA is or is not successfully demonstrating. Again as mentioned above, only the way the question is asked the second time counts toward the points.

References

Schoenberg, I. E. (1986) *Talk about trivia: 1001 questions*. White Plains, NY: Longman.

Presentation Summaries—Take Two!

Barbara Thompson
Princeton University

GOALS
To deliver a direct and concise 2-minute summary of a previous 5- to 8-minute presentation

PREPARATION TIME
None

EXECUTION TIME
3 minutes per student

ASSUMPTIONS
Participants will have given a 5- to 8-minute videotaped presentation in class before they do this activity.

RESOURCES
Recording equipment

Introduction

One of the most difficult language tasks for nonnative speaking students to master is the skill of communicating in a direct and concise manner. In this activity, students learn to extract the most salient points from a longer piece of discourse to summarize a previous presentation or lesson effectively. This is an important pedagogical skill for ITAs to develop. Students also target three specific areas that they want to improve from their original presentation. By selecting achievable improvement goals for their summaries, students are able to see progress, which is very motivating.

Procedure

1. Students meet in tutorials with their instructors to review videotapes of their five- to eight-minute in-class presentations.

2. During the tutorial, students identify three areas they would like to improve in their presentation summaries. These areas must be specific and achievable (i.e., more eye contact, correct pronunciation of key words, monitoring specific phonemes, or more direct responses to questions).

3. At home, students prepare and practice the two-minute summaries of their previous presentations out loud.

4. Students have two minutes to present their videotaped summaries in class and answer one question from the audience.

5. Students watch the video of the summary with their instructors to evaluate how successful they were in presenting the main points of their original presentation clearly and concisely.

6. For homework, students watch their tapes and comment in writing on the extent to which they improved in each of the three areas they selected.

Working with Authentic TA Discourse

Janet Goodwin

University of California–Los Angeles

GOALS

To familiarize ITAs with the discourse they need to accomplish typical TA communication tasks

PREPARATION TIME

Varies, depending on whether existing transcripts are used or created by recording TAs on campus

EXECUTION TIME

2–3 class periods

RESOURCES

Transcripts of real TA discourse (preferably accompanied by video and/or audio recordings) representing your ITA participants' fields

Introduction

Given the flexibility and rich vocabulary of the English language, international students are often understandably intimidated by the linguistic demands of classroom teaching. Using the technique described here, these students can start to learn and collect the conventional expressions used in such activities as small talk, introducing and concluding a lesson, fielding questions, handling wrong answers, giving instructions, assigning homework, and moving from one point to another.

Preparation

1. To provide the real TA discourse that is needed as the springboard for this activity, obtain or create transcripts of classroom or laboratory interactions involving students and experienced TAs from appropriate disciplines. The most productive, but time-consuming, approach is to visit classrooms, laboratories, and discussion sections to record TAs (either native speakers or highly proficient second language speakers) on your campus and create transcripts of your recordings. This do-it-yourself approach is complicated and time consuming, but has the benefit of providing you with a deeper understanding of different disciplinary communication cultures. A

sample subject permission form can be found at www.iei.uiuc.edu/ TESOL/subjperm.html. If you are unable to record TAs on your campus, you can obtain transcripts from several disciplines on this web site.

2. Choose one communicative function as a focus (e.g., introducing a lesson) and analyze the transcripts to identify conventional discourse patterns that occur over several instructors and disciplines. (Ideally, you need at least three to four examples of TAs performing a task.) These linguistic patterns provide the "meat" of this technique. For each recording, transcribe the minute or two that is devoted to your discourse focus. The following procedure highlights the discourse patterns typical of introducing a lesson as the focus.

Procedure

1. Observation task (outside of class) for consciousness-raising:
   - Students observe two or three TAs in their department and note the language they use to introduce the topic of the lesson.
   - Students report their observations either through online discussion board postings or in-class discussions.

2. Analysis task:
   - In or out of class, students analyze the instructor-generated transcripts to highlight the language patterns that the TAs use to introduce a lesson. The highlighted language is listed on the board.

3. Presentation of linguistic patterns:
   - Following student analysis, the instructor presents an organized list of the common linguistic patterns found in the transcripts and compares it to the examples found by the students in Steps 1 and 2. Grammatical patterns and common vocabulary are discussed. The list for introducing a lesson, for example, might look like this:

Let's	First of all, *let's talk about* . . .
	OK, *let's get to work.* What'll we tackle first?
	I think I can anticipate your questions so *let's just kind of go through it* quickly.
Gonna/going to	We're *gonna talk about* . . .
	Today we're *gonna look at* how . . .
	So that's what we're *gonna do* today.
	I'm *gonna cover* some of the ways . . .
	So I'm *gonna go ahead and get started.*
Wanna/want to	Today I *wanna talk about* . . .
	What I *wanna go over* today is . . .
	I *wanna focus on* two major points today . . .

4. Listening and viewing task (in class):
   - While looking at the transcripts, students watch/listen to each recorded segment in which a TA introduces his or her lesson. Focusing on one listening task at a time (e.g., patterns in pausing, accented syllables, or intonation patterns), the students are asked to mark their transcripts. This task involves listening to each one-to two-minute segment several times.
   - Using an overhead transparency of the transcript, the instructor elicits the pauses, prominent syllables, and most salient intonation patterns. In this way, students can check their answers.

5. Mini-lesson task (in class):
   - Students prepare a one- to two-minute class introduction to a discipline-appropriate lesson, incorporating the linguistic patterns they have learned in the earlier steps.
   - These introductions are recorded by the instructor for students to view outside of class, either in a media laboratory or on the course web site.
   - Either in class or after viewing the recorded introductions, students complete a simple peer evaluation form answering questions such as What did this person do well? and What suggestions for improvement can you make?

6. Self-evaluation task (completed outside of class):
   - Students listen to their recorded introductions and make a transcript (printed, double-spaced) to hand in.
   - Students fill out a self-evaluation form with questions such as the following:
     - How did you introduce the lesson? Highlight the linguistic patterns on your transcript.
     - Describe your body language (if video was used).
     - Did you notice any aspects of your pronunciation or fluency that could be improved?
     - Did you notice any grammar or word choice errors?
     - What did you learn from the peer feedback?
     - What did you learn from watching the video?
   - The instructor provides feedback on similar aspects of the presentation.

RESOURCES

Books

Angelo, T. A., & Cross, K. P. (1993). *Classroom assessment techniques: A handbook for college teachers* (2nd ed.). San Francisco, CA: Jossey-Bass.

Bain, K. (2004). *What the best college teachers do.* Cambridge, MA: Harvard University Press.

Bonwell, C. C. (1996). Enhancing the lecture: Revitalizing a traditional format. In T. E. Sutherland & C. C. Bonwell (Eds.), *New directions for teaching and learning: No. 67. Using active learning in college classes: A range of options for faculty* (pp. 31–44). San Francisco, CA: Jossey-Bass.

Brownworth, B., & Kaufman, D. (2006). *Case studies in ITA development.* Alexandria, VA: Teachers of English to Speakers of Other Languages.

Committee on Undergraduate Science Education. (1997). *Science teaching reconsidered: A handbook.* Washington, DC: National Academy Press.

Cook, A. (2000). *American accent training: A guide to speaking and pronouncing American English for everyone who speaks English as a second language* (2nd ed.). Hauppauge, NY: Barron's.

Curzan, A., & Damour, L. (2000). *First day to final grade: A graduate student's guide to teaching.* Ann Arbor, MI: University of Michigan.

Davis, B. G. (1993). *Tools for teaching.* San Francisco, CA: Jossey-Bass.

Erickson, B. L., Peters, C. B., & Strommer, D. W. (2006). *Teaching first-year college students* (Rev. & expanded ed.). San Francisco, CA: Jossey-Bass.

Goodwin, J. (2005). The power of context in teaching pronunciation. In J. Frodesen & C. Holten (Eds.), *The power of context in language teaching and learning.* Boston, MA: Heinle & Heinle.

Hahn, L. D., & Dickerson, W. B. (1999). *Speechcraft: Discourse pronunciation for advanced learners.* Ann Arbor, MI: University of Michigan Press.

Haynes, C. (Ed.). (2002). *Innovations in interdisciplinary teaching.* Westport, CT: Greenwood Press.

Huba, M. E., & Freed, J. E. (2000). *Learner-centered assessment on college campuses: Shifting the focus from teaching to learning.* Boston, MA: Allyn & Bacon.

King, K. (1999). *The big picture: Idioms as metaphors.* Boston, MA: Houghton Mifflin.

Klein, J. T. (1990). *Interdisciplinarity: History, theory, and practice.* Detroit, MI: Wayne State University Press.

Lambert, L., & Tice, S. L. (Eds.). (1993). *Preparing graduate students to teach: A guide to programs that improve undergraduate education and develop tomorrow's faculty.* Sterling, VA: Stylus.

Leki, I. (1992). *Understanding ESL writers: A guide for teachers.* Portsmouth, NH: Boynton/Cook.

Madden, C. G., & Myers, C. L. (Eds.). (1994*). Discourse and performance of international teaching assistants.* Alexandria, VA: Teachers of English to Speakers of Other Languages.

Marincovich, M., Prostko, J., & Stout, F. (Eds.). (1998). *The professional development of graduate teaching assistants.* Bolton, MA: Anker.

Matsuda, P. K., Cox, M., Jordan, J., & Ortmeier-Hooper, C. (2005). *Second language writing in the composition classroom: A critical sourcebook.* Boston, MA: Bedford/St. Martin's.

Meyers, C., & Holt, S. (2001). *Pronunciation for success: Student workbook* (2nd ed.). Burnsville, MN: Aspen Productions.

Miller, S. F. (2005). *Targeting pronunciation: Communicating clearly in English* (2nd ed.). Boston, MA: Houghton Mifflin.

Nyquist, J. D., & Wulff, D. H. (1996). *Working effectively with graduate assistants.* Thousand Oaks, CA: Sage.

Sarosy, P., & Sherak, K. (2006). *Lecture ready 1: Strategies for academic listening, note-taking, and discussion.* New York, NY: Oxford University Press.

Smith, J., Meyers, C. M., & Burkhalter, A. J. (1992). *Communicate: Strategies for international teaching assistants.* Englewood, NJ: Regents/Prentice-Hall.

Swales, J. M., & Feak, C. B. (2004). *Academic writing for graduate students: Essential tasks and skills.* Ann Arbor, MI: University of Michigan Press.

Wennerstrom, A. (1989). *Techniques for teachers: A guide for nonnative speakers of English.* Ann Arbor, MI: University of Michigan Press.

Zamel, V., & Spack, R. (Eds.). (2004). *Crossing the curriculum: Multilingual learners in college classrooms.* Mahwah, NJ: Lawrence Erlbaum Associates.

Zull, J. E. (2002). *The art of changing the brain: Enriching the practice of teaching by exploring the biology of learning.* Sterling, VA: Stylus.

Articles

Benesch, S. (1996, Winter). Needs analysis and curriculum development in EAP: An example of a critical approach. *TESOL Quarterly, 30*(4), 723–728.

Douglas, D., & Myers, C. (1989). TAs on TV: Demonstrating communication strategies for international teaching assistants. *English for specific purposes, 8*(2), 169–179.

Felder, R. M., & Brent, R. (1996, Spring). Navigating the bumpy road to student-centered instruction. *College Teaching, 44*(2), 43–47.

Harklau, L. (1994, Summer). ESL and mainstream classes: Contrasting second language learning contexts. *TESOL Quarterly, 28*(2), 241–272.

Lu, M.-Z., & Matsuda, P. K. (Eds.). (2006, July). Cross-language relations in composition [Special issue]. *College English, 68*(6).

Mansilla, V. B. (2005, January/February). Assessing student work at disciplinary crossroads. *Change, 37*(1), 14–21.

Films

Derek Bok Center for Teaching and Learning (Producer). (1999). *How to speak* [Film]. Cambridge, MA: Harvard University.

Derek Bok Center for Teaching and Learning (Producer). (1993). *Teaching in America* [Film]. Cambridge, MA: Harvard University.

Derek Bok Center for Teaching and Learning (Producer). (1993). *What students want* [Film]. Cambridge, MA: Harvard University.

Douglas, D., & Myers, C. (Producers). (1990). *Teaching assistant communication strategies* [Video and instructor's manual]. Ames, IA: Iowa State University, Media Production Unit.

Herreid, C. F. (Producer). (2002) *Team learning: Cooperative learning in the science classroom* [Video]. Buffalo, NY: State University of New York at Buffalo.

Herreid, C. F. (Producer). (2002). *The use of case studies and group discussions in science education* [Video]. Buffalo, NY: State University of New York at Buffalo.

Institute for Teaching and Learning (Producer). (2001). *Respect on the line* [Video]. Storrs, CT: University of Connecticut.

Web Sites

Authentic Assessment Toolbox
http://jonathan.mueller.faculty.noctrl.edu/toolbox/

Case Study Teaching Videos
http://ublib.buffalo.edu/libraries/projects/cases/teaching/videos/video.html

English Trailers
www.english-trailers.com/index.php

Guide to Scoring LEP Student Responses to Open-Ended Mathematics Items
www3.ksde.org/sfp/esol/guide_math.pdf

The Meta-Profession Project
www.cedanet.com/meta/

Myths and Misconceptions About Second Language Learning
www.ncela.gwu.edu/pubs/ncrcdsll/epr5.htm

POD–IDEA Center Learning Notes
http://idea.ksu.edu/podidea/index_learning.html

POD–IDEA Center Notes
http://idea.ksu.edu/podidea/index.html

Resources in Science and Engineering Education
www.ncsu.edu/felder-public/RMF.html

Teaching at Stanford
http://ctl.stanford.edu/handbook.pdf

Teaching Engineering
https://engineering.purdue.edu/ChE/News_and_Events/Publications/
    teaching_engineering/index.html

Teaching Strategies and Disciplinary Resources
www.crlt.umich.edu/tstrategies/teachings.html

Teaching with Writing
http://writing.umn.edu/tww/nonnative/nonnative_index.htm

Writing Matters
http://mwp01.mwp.hawaii.edu/resources/wm6.htm

INDEX

FERPA (Family Educational
Rights and Privacy Act), 44
Ferris Bueller's Day Off, 106
fielding questions, 146, 148, 163
foregrounding, 153
free-response, 4
Freisem, K., xiv, 52

gambits, 39
gender, 21, 28, 101, 130
gestures, 40, 118, 120, 127, 159
Gibber, J., xiv, 88
Goodwin, J., xiv, 156, 163, 168
Gourlay, B., xv, 98, 144, 148, 150
*Graduate Student Instructor
Guidebook,* 21
Greek alphabet, 150, 152
Grooters, S., viii, xv, 24, 35
group dynamics, 55, 74
group work, 6, 14, 74
GSI (Graduate Student
Instructor), 82

Halbert, A., xv, 128
*A Handbook for Faculty
Development,* 64
*Handbook of College Teaching:
Theory and Applications,* 23
*Handbook of Intercultural
Training,* 106
Hannah, J., xv, 48
Harvard, xii, xx, xxi, 58, 146,
167, 170
high school, 111, 113, 115
"How to Enhance Learning by
Using High-Stakes and Low-
Stakes Writing," 37

identity, 21, 101
idioms, 113, 120, 124, 127, 144
immigrant students, 13
impromptu speaking, 39, 137
interdisciplinary, 68
international undergraduate
students, 13
intonation, 118, 136, 155, 156,
165

Jigsaw, 6, 19, 144
Johns Hopkins University, xx,
xxii, 60, 101, 142, 158

Kane, S. K., xv, 48
Kenyon, K., xvi, 136, 153

lab
computer, 48
group dynamics, 55
instruction, 52, 53
large classes, 84
Lawrence, M., xvi, 24, 139, 169
learning online, 70
learning styles, 18, 128
lecture, 11, 14, 19, 76, 118
Liptak, C., xvi, 103
Lost in Translation, 120

Marincovich, M., xvi, 62, 168
Massachusetts Institute of
Technology (MIT), xi, xiii,
xix, xx, xxvi, 28, 39, 74
McCabe, A. P., xvii, 60
McClure, N. C., xvii, 6
McKeachie's Teaching Tips, 37
mentors, 4, 62
Meyers, C., xvii, 103, 168, 169